Preparing for the Future

Notes and Queries for Concerned Educators

Books of related interest also published by Adamantine

Into the 21st Century: A Handbook for a Sustainable Future
Brian Burrows, Alan Mayne, and Paul Newbury

Journalism in the 21st Century: Online Information, Electronic Databases, and the News
Tom Koch

Technoculture and Change: Strategic Solutions for Tomorrow's Society
D. N. Chorafas and E. M. Binder

Inventing the Future: Reflections on Science, Technology and Nature
David Suzuki

The Next Three Futures: Paradigms of Things To Come
W. Warren Wagar

Visions for the 21st Century
Sheila M. Moorcroft (ed)

Crucial Questions About the Future
Allen Tough

Nature, Technology, and Society: Cultural Roots of the Current Environmental Crisis
Victor Ferkiss

A Short History of the Future
W. Warren Wagar

Resources for the Future: An International Annotated Bibliography for the 21st Century
Alan Mayne

Creative Compartments: A Design for Future Organisation
Gerard Fairtlough

Groupware in the 21st Century
Peter Lloyd (ed)

Vitality and Renewal: A Manager's Guide for the 21st Century
Colin Hutchinson

Framing the Future: A 21st Century Reader
Bruce Lloyd (ed)

Preparing for the Future

Notes and Queries for Concerned Educators

Edited by
David Hicks

ADAMANTINE PRESS LIMITED

Published in the United Kingdom in 1994
by Adamantine Press Limited
3 Henrietta Street
Covent Garden
London WC2E 8LU
England

Composed in Palatino 11 on 13 by Intype, London

British Cataloguing in Publication Data

A full catalogue record for this book is available from the British Library.
(Adamantine Studies on the 21st Century, ISSN 0954–6103; v. no. 12)

ISBN 0–7449–0107–3 cloth
0–7449–0108–1 Paper

Printed in Great Britain at the University Press, Cambridge.

A volume in the series
Adamantine Studies on the 21st Century

'Leadership & Learning' strand
(strand editor: Bruce Lloyd)

Published in association with the World Wide Fund for Nature.

For the Children

The rising hills, the slopes
of statistics
lie before us.
the steep climb
of everything, going up,
up, as we all
go down.

In the next century
or the one beyond that,
they say,
are valleys, pastures,
we can meet there in
peace
if we make it.

To climb these coming
crests
one word to you, to
you and your children:

stay together
learn the flowers
go light.

Gary Snyder

(from *Turtle Island*, New Directions Books, New York, 1974)

CONTENTS

FOREWORD

by Francis Kinsman
Visiting Fellow in 21st Century Studies
Brunel University

Educare – to educate. To 'lead out', from the Latin root; in other words, to drag forth, encourage and celebrate with garlands the talents of the next generation, so that all these sparkling new people may feel allowed to fulfil themselves – and manifest the wonderful potential of their possible society.

Fond dream, say the negativists.

And yet. It *does* move, as Galileo groaned, even while he was under torture from the Inquisition. Even under today's torture, education does move. The unique human spirit is not going to knuckle under to the dead hand of the drab collective. But in order to move in the right direction, it *does* need, from well-wishers, the encouragement and celebration of its movement.

It had better get it, or we are all in dire trouble. From dedicated teachers, trainers and educators it can and probably will get it. Even though the bloody-minded determination to dish the whole process may sometimes seem to be all-pervading, the positive message can nonetheless shine through: it requires only that enough innovative educationalists, creative teachers, interested parents, and lively pupils *have some sense of the future of the educational process.*

A tallish order, but as this book demonstrates, by no means an impossible one. It is a matter of enthusing children with an idea of their own futures, and with the sense that they are in control of them. It is also a matter of enthusing parents and teachers with the idea that they can combine to bring this urgent possibility about.

Young people are much more imaginative than adults as a general rule. They understand myths, even potentially rather disturbing myths, better than their elders. Similarly, they understand futures, even rather disastrous futures, better than them, too. We can learn from this but, more importantly, we have to learn to let them have their heads as far as their own futures are concerned. One half of all scientific knowledge has been assimilated over the past 30 years; one half of all scientists have been working since the past 25. Move over, dinosaurs . . . !

It is therefore vastly important that education is directed towards the way things are going to be, rather than towards the way they were. For example, the training of and focus on the right hemisphere of the brain – the intuitive, creative part – will become as, if not more, crucial to the successful person of tomorrow than will traditional nous. The logical, numerate, word-perfect part emanating from the brain's left hemisphere may well be overtaken by, or at the very least harnessed to, the computer within the next fifty years.

Glorious human wildness may be all that there is left for us to glory in. As T. S. Eliot put it, 'where is the wisdom we have lost in knowledge; where is the knowledge we have lost in information?' Had he been a computer programmer rather than a bank clerk, he might have added, 'where is the information we have lost in data?'

Tomorrow's adults will have to come to terms with a rate of change that is unprecedented in human history. This being so, all educators have from this minute onwards to be unbelievably sensitive as to the demands that are going to be placed upon their charges. They will have to introduce them to the realities of this computerised and networked world, which is both 'high-tech' and incorporates the human dimension of what has been called 'high touch'.

In this, one has to discount the angry but understandable reaction that computerisation and the electronic revolution are agents for dehumanising humanity, however. Instead, they can release human beings to concentrate on the main functions for which they were placed on this earth to fulfil; the wonders of creativity, of intuition, of artistry and (dare one breathe it), of love – that are at the very core of our shared being.

Certainly, educators will have to keep one step ahead of their pupils in the realms of technology, but certainly also, they will have to keep a thousand miles ahead of them in the realms of the depth of human experience and of its essential, ethical interdependence. And yet 'the journey of a thousand miles begins only with one step'. Paradoxically, it seems that these two characteristics of humanity are becoming visibly inter-related, and that the sublime 'inner marriage' of the masculine and feminine principles of the human condition is at last tantalisingly accessible, after all the aeons of our evolution.

At the same time, chaos theory is now being translated into chaos practice; our terrifying and brilliant destiny now stands before us. Education is without any doubt the most crucial aspect of our mutual future in such a time of change. *Educare* – we simply must lead and tease out that undiscovered talent, of whatever kind and wherever we come across it.

Please let us all acknowledge, then, with an unlikely combination of humility and power, our part in working with young people; in gently but surely learning to reassemble our building blocks together, to construct a more appropriate civilisation for them and their successors.

Chapter 1

INTRODUCTION

> You must give birth to your images
> They are the future waiting to be born
> – Rilke

The 21st century will be very different from today and yet study of the future is a neglected issue in education. Young people are concerned about a range of current global issues but also often feel unprepared for what the future may bring. If all education is for the future then the future needs to be a more explicit concern at all levels of education.

In a world where change is increasingly rapid, whether at local, national or global scales, it is important to ask questions about the future. Where are we going and where do we want to go? What are our hopes and dreams for the future, for ourselves, for others and for the planet? And what can we do together *now* to help create a more just and sustainable future?

A crucial time in history

Teachers today live at a crucial time in the history of the planet, the last decade of the twentieth century approaching the third millennium. These are times of rapid and often confusing change: the collapse of the Soviet Union, war in the Balkans, famine in

Africa, the increasing gap between rich and poor, depletion of the ozone layer, drastic loss of plant and animal species. As Sandra Postel writes:

> Eliminating these threats to our future requires a fundamental restructuring of many elements of society – a shift from fossil fuels to efficient, solar-based energy systems, new transportation networks and city designs that lessen automobile use, redistribution of land and wealth, equality between the sexes in all cultures, and a rapid transition to smaller families. It demands reduced consumption of resources by the rich to make room for higher living standards for the poor. And with current notions of economic growth at the root of so much of the earth's ecological deterioration, it calls for a rethinking of our basic values and vision of progress.[1]

If these are some of the changes that are needed what should education for the 21st century look like? What do our students need to know, what skills must they develop, if we are to help them create such a future? Both teachers and teacher educators, whether knowingly or not, are managers of long term change. As Dean Inge of St Pauls wrote in 1929 'the proper time to influence the character of children is about a hundred years before they are born.'

Education for the future

No form of education can be neutral or value-free. All educational legislation, policies, resources and practice, embody particular values about the nature of education and the process of learning. At least three quite distinct, although sometimes overlapping, traditions can be identified – the utilitarian, the liberal and the reconstructionist.

The utilitarian tradition sees the main task of education as equipping students to fit into existing social situations. It tends to stress formal classroom management within a highly structured and often centralised curriculum. The liberal tradition is more broadly concerned with preparing students to participate in all aspects of life. There is a stress on self-actualisation via less formal classroom management and a more flexible curriculum. The reconstructionist tradition takes a socially-critical stand which recognises both how schools reflect society and how education can be used to transform the structures of daily life. Such an approach invites critical reflection and action for change both inside and outside the classroom.[2]

Environmental educators have long argued that a socially-critical orientation must underpin any notion of education *for* the environment.[3] Given the situation described by Postel above the same has to be said for any notion of education *for* the future. The fact that we need an education specifically orientated towards the future should be clear to all those with a responsibility for education.

> Anyone who reads newspapers, listens to the radio, or watches television knows – or at least senses – that civilisation is in trouble . . . We have inadvertently acquired a great deal of influence over the future habitability of the planet. At issue is whether we can assume the responsibility to go with it. In many respects, this is the question for our generation. If we cannot reverse the trends that are undermining our future, environmental deterioration and economic decline may soon start to feed on each other, depriving future generations of the opportunity to support themselves.[4]

Educating for the future requires that we help both students and teachers to develop skills of foresight, that is the ability to anticipate and be more pro-active to change. Given the speed and complexity of current social, political and technological change, we need to be able to look critically well into the 21st century. All actions, all acts of producing and consuming, have consequences in future time. By definition these are consequences that we cannot immediately see, but more careful consideration of possible consequences means that future generations will benefit rather than be harmed by our actions in the present.[5] By recognising that there is not one future but many alternative futures the question of choice is constantly raised. Becoming aware of the wide range of choices can lead to more responsible and thoughtful decision making in the present.

Using this book

This book is intended for all those working in teacher education who take an interest in the future of their profession and the future of the planet. It is for all those who take an interest in the welfare of future generations, whether children in school now or those not yet born. It contains a selection of key writings on the future and on education for the future. These include the need for such an education (chapter 2), some background to the futures field (chapter 3), the importance of images of the future (chapter 4), the need to envision preferable futures (chapter 5), the nature of sustainable futures (chapter 6), and some examplar teaching/learning activities (chapter 7). It is the first time that such writings have been brought together in this way for teacher educators.

The book is not intended to be a comprehensive text on education for the future. Rather it is a series of introductory notes and queries for teacher educators which compliment a range of other available resources.[6] The first five chapters provide a series of basic readings which can be used to assist course design and delivery. They can be used by both tutors and students and each concludes with a series of practical questions for follow-up work. These focus both on the student's own learning and also the way in which futures thinking can enhance both National Curriculum subjects and the cross-curricular themes. They attempt to link both theory and practice and can be used for seminar, tutorial and written work.

In chapter 2 David Hicks raises a series of key questions for educators prompted by the 1992 Earth Summit and the approaching millenium. He sets out both a rationale for education for the future and some of the current global trends that are likely to influence the lives of children now in school. In particular he stresses the need to identify desirable futures and to listen to a wide range of voices on the future. In chapter 3 Hicks goes on to illustrate, from his own experience, how concern for the future can come to be generated. He describes the broader educational context for classroom initiatives and the work of the Global Futures Project in this field.

Rick Slaughter in chapter 4 focuses on changing images of the future in the the twentieth century. He looks at the rise of dystopian (negative) images of futures and what appears to be a cultural decline in imaging capacity. This is followed, however, by consideration of a variety of ways in which this dilemma can be addressed. He concludes that there is in fact a substantive basis for informed optimism and empowerment.

In chapter 5 Elise Boulding focuses on the critical importance of being able to envision more peaceful futures. Due to the difficulty of generating positive images of the future during the nuclear age she collaborated with Warren Ziegler to develop an experimental futures workshop. The procedures for this are described together with examples of positive imagery and their possible relationship to preparedness for social action.

Lester Brown in chapter 6 asks what picture of the future is needed to guide our actions towards a global community that can endure. Since 'successfully structuring a sustainable society requires that we have some vision of what it would look like' he sets out his assumptions and then sketches in the parameters of just such a society. We need many more such scenarios at global, national and local levels.

The final chapter contains six detailed practical activities for use with students. They all share a common format of: purpose, preparation and procedure. Each focuses on different aspects of education for the future. Trends for the Future gives students the opportunity to debate the likely importance of different trends on life in the 21st century. Global Timelines provides an opportunity to explore student's own feelings about probable and preferable futures for the planet. Preferable Futures focuses on the need to identify particular goals or indicators for a better world and to examine what these would look like in daily life. Future Thinking asks what many of these ideas look like when applied to the National Curriculum and the cross-curricular themes. Sustainable Futures raises some initial questions about the interrelated elements of sustainability. Finally Envisioning the Future by Elise Boulding sets out a procedure for identifying the key elements of preferable futures.

If pupils in school now have a legal entitlement to preparation 'for the opportunities, responsibilities and experiences of adult life'[7] there is much that teacher educators need to do. That adult life for which pupils need to be prepared will stretch well into the latter half of the 21st century. Only an explicit and critical education for the future can fully deliver that entitlement.

Chapter 2

RECLAIMING THE FUTURE: WHAT EVERY EDUCATOR NEEDS TO KNOW

David Hicks

The children we teach in school now will spend most of their lives in the 21st century. Those leaving school in the 1990s will become the parents, voters, workers, business people and visionaries of tomorrow. If all education is for the future, where is the future in education? *How* are we preparing students for those responsibilities? *How* are we helping them to think more critically and creatively about the future?

My argument is that as educators, and particularly as environmental educators, we need to engage in the task of 'reclaiming the future'. I will illustrate this with reference to: i) the approaching millennium; ii) the need to educate more explicitly for the future; iii) the importance of being able to envision more just and sustainable futures; and iv) some thoughts on moving forwards.

Approaching the millennium

A symbolic threshold

When I began teaching about global issues in the late-60s I can remember asking my students to work out how old they would be in the year 2000. The date seemed very remote, but important, and even then symbolic as some sort of turning point. Now it is much closer and even more compelling, this culture-bound temporal coordinate. When we reach the year 2000, or to be more precise 2001, the last decade of a century turns into a first, the 20th century changes into the 21st, and the second millennium into the third. These are powerful metaphors of change.

In the biblical millennium heaven could only be established on earth after the final clash between good and evil and for some the modern millennium prompts similar questions – will it be the Golden Age or the Apocalypse?

> It was the best of times, it was the worst of times, it was the age of wisdom, it was the age of foolishness, it was the epoch of belief, it was the epoch of incredulity, it was the season of Light, it was the season of Darkness, it was the spring of hope, it was the winter of despair, we had everything before us, we had nothing before us . . .

The opening paragraph of Dickens' *A Tale of Two Cities* was written to describe the 1790s. It could equally have been written about the 1990s.

What the millennium can provide is a mirror for the deep human need we have to make historical sense of both personal and cultural change. It is well suited to do this being a rare event in recorded human history. Once an event is perceived as a turning point or threshold it often becomes invested with a symbolic power which heightens the quest for new meaning and new beginnings. When and where in our teaching, I wonder, do we encourage students to share *their* feelings about this time?

Earth in the balance

In 1992, just before the 'Earth Summit' in Rio, the *Guardian* ran the headline 'Earth's future in the balance, say top scientists.' It referred to a joint report from the US National Academy of

Sciences and the 'normally-conservative' Royal Society of London, which warned of the catastrophic consequences of resource consumption, environmental destruction and population growth.

> In essence, the two bodies – to which both governments have always turned for advice on scientific matters – have endorsed many of the warnings issued over the past 20 years by pressure groups such as Friends of the Earth and Greenpeace, making it difficult for politicians to say scientific opinion is divided, or that talk of global disaster is scaremongering.[1]

Twenty years ago the 'limits to growth' debate was sparked off by publication of the first report from the Club of Rome. The authors of that report, which predicted global collapse if present trends continued, have now published a sequel called *Beyond the Limits*.[2] Whilst they argue that the world has already overshot some limits, they also show that a sustainable future *is* technically and economically feasible. When and where in our teaching do we encourage students to debate such issues?

Thinking about the future

We spend a large part of our time thinking about the future. Identifying our goals for the future enhances our ability to work in the present, adds to our motivation and helps give us direction. Whilst on the one hand the future is intangible, it is also of crucial importance, human existence cannot be conceived of without it.

Yet because there are no facts about the future we often neglect it or leave it to others: management, economists, politicians, multinational corporations, and its *their* future that we finish up with. We often know what we *don't* want in the future, but may be less clear about what we *do* want. We are also more used to thinking about personal rather than societal or global futures.

The times now require that we think much more explicitly about the future and about how local and global futures are interrelated. In particular we need to ask the questions, where are we going and where do we *want* to go, locally, nationally and globally? Nearly twenty years ago Alvin Toffler wrote:

> All education springs from images of the future and all education creates images of the future. Thus all education, whether so intended or not, is a preparation for the future. Unless we

> understand the future for which we are preparing we may do tragic damage to those we teach.[3]

Indeed there is no such thing as the future (singular), for at any given moment in time any number of futures (plural) are possible. The term 'alternative futures' or simply 'futures' is thus often used as a shorthand reminder of this.

For any exploration of alternative futures to be of use it needs to be remembered that different people and groups have quite different views of the future: a middle class child in Perth, a homeless woman in London, an unemployed worker in Dresden or a logger in Brazil. Clearly some groups in society also have much more power than others to define the future, generally those who are rich in the global system or who wield power through, say, transnational corporations, international banking, governments, the military, the media. In some sense such groups also colonise the future, particularly big business with its constant creation of new 'needs' for tomorrow.

What we expect in the future is often not what we would wish for. Helping pupils identify both their probable and preferable futures is an essential element of preparation for adult life. Teaching only about problems can alienate young people. Learning about possible alternatives and proposed solutions is much more likely to motivate them. The current state of the planet requires that exploration of just and sustainable futures becomes a major priority at all levels of society. If we can work to envision such futures with others then we stand a better chance of bringing them about. Future generations would surely ask no less of us than this.

Educating for the future

Children's interests

Research from the Henley Centre for Forecasting in the UK shows that young people in school *are* very aware of, and concerned about, global issues.[4] In particular they see the environment as a key concern, with destruction of the ozone layer, deforestation, global warming, CFCs and endangered species as the problems most urgently requiring attention. Generally children show a high level of interest in environmental issues, with school lessons and projects being cited as their main source of information. However over 60% of the children surveyed still said they didn't think enough was taught about the environment at school. They are very aware that the future holds both promise and threat.

Clarifying the rationale

In a society or time period where change occurs slowly it can generally be assumed that the future will be very similar to the present. However, in periods when change is much more rapid, the future becomes more uncertain and unpredictable. The 19th and 20th centuries have been just such a period, with rapid economic, technological and political change. We live in times of uncertainty and surprise. 'Now' is the place where we need to anticipate and prepare for the future before it unfolds.

The purpose of 'education for the future' is to enable pupils to explore various scenarios which may emerge from current trends and to explore the implications of these. Once we realise that we cannot 'opt out' of the future it takes on a radically new meaning. All actions and choices, including choices *not* to act or choose, have future consequences. Rick Slaughter writes:

> We cannot alter the past, but we have common interests in achieving life-preserving, sustainable futures. It follows that a central task for teachers is to explore with their pupils some of the major problems and possibilities that lie ahead and thereby sensitise them to the implications of choices and actions in the present.[5]

Education for the future clarifies the range of alternatives, which then give rise to wider choices, which can lead to more responsible action in the present. The rationale for including a clearer futures dimension in the curriculum would include the following points.

Table 1 – Rationale for a futures dimension in the curriculum

1. *Pupil motivation*
   Pupil expectation about the future can affect behaviour in the present, e.g. that something is, or is not, worth working for. Clear images of desired personal goals can help stimulate motivation and achievement.

2. *Anticipating change*
   Anticipatory skills and flexibility of mind are important in times of rapid change. Such skills enable pupils to deal more effectively with uncertainty and to initiate, rather than merely respond to, change.

3. *Critical thinking*
   In weighing up information, considering trends and imagining alternatives, pupils will need to exercise reflective and critical thinking. This is often triggered by realising the contradictions between how the world is now and how one would like it to be.

4. *Clarifying values*
   All images of the future are underpinned by differing value assumptions about human nature and society. In a democratic society pupils need to be able to begin to identify such value judgements before they can themselves make appropriate choices between alternatives.

5. *Decision making*
   Becoming more aware of trends and events which are likely to influence one's future and investigating the possible consequences of one's actions on others in the future, leads to more thoughtful decision making in the present.

6. *Creative imagination*
   One faculty that can contribute to, and which is particularly enhanced by, designing alternative futures is that of the creative imagination. Both this *and* critical thinking are need to envision a range of preferable futures from the personal to the global.

7. *A better world*
   It is important in a democratic society that young people develop their sense of vision particularly in relation to more just and sustainable futures. Such forward looking thinking is an essential ingredient in both the preserving and improving of society.

8. *Responsible citizenship*
   Critical participation in democratic life leads to the development of political skills and thus more active and responsible

citizenship. Future generations are then more likely to benefit, rather than lose, from decisions made today.

Trends for the future

Whilst on the one hand the future *is* unknown, one of the tasks of futurists is to analyse social, political and economic trends and to try and gauge their possible future impact on society. In that sense the major problems of today will continue to be amongst the major issues of tomorrow. Some crucial global trends are shown in Table 2. These are partly based on Naisbitt's *Megatrends 2000*.[6] His actual analysis of these trends, however, is both shallow and ethnocentric.

Table 2 – Some trends for the future

1. *Cultural diversity*
   Whilst we are now all part of one global system, it is ethnic, cultural and historical differences amongst peoples that will increasingly influence national and global affairs in the future.

2. *The Pacific rim*
   The centre of world trade is now shifting from the Atlantic to the Pacific rim. Asian countries bordering the Pacific will become more important as they undergo the fastest period of economic expansion in history.

3. *Women in leadership*
   Women are now increasingly taking up leadership roles in business, especially in the U.S. This trend is likely to spread and will have a significant impact on the way in which business is organised in the future.

4. *Biotechnology*
   The new scientific frontier of genetic engineering is about to transform our lives, whether we like it or not. This includes both the creation of new plant and animal breeds as well as alteration of human genes.

5. *Religious revival*
   There are now clear signs of a worldwide religious and spiritual revival. This ranges from the growth of fundamentalist and

evangelical groups to the spread of New Age beliefs and a renaissance of more ancient spiritual traditions.

6. *Environmental concern*
   Due to issues such as global warming and ozone depletion there is now an upsurge of popular interest in environmental issues, particularly in the rich world. Increasingly people are aware of the need to preserve and nurture the planet itself.

7. *Wealth and poverty*
   The nature of the world economic system is such that the gap between the countries of the North and South will continue to increase. This growing division will create serious future problems both between and within countries.

8. *Changing worldviews*
   In the West there are some signs of a new value shift away from a predominantly scientific and mechanistic view of the world to a more holistic and ecological one. This can be seen in many fields of enquiry, from health care and the new physics to psychology and education.

When and where in our teaching do we encourage students to discuss the possible impact of such trends on their own lives, and on the lives of others, in the 21st century?

For those who would like to study the futures field more deeply I would recommend Warren Wagar's *The Next Three Futures: Paradigms of Things to Come* and Michael Marien's *What I Have Learned: Thinking About the Future Then and Now*.[7] There are, of course, also specialist journals such as *Futures* and *Futures Research Quarterly*.[8]

Envisioning the future

Images of the future

One of the most valuable distinctions that futurists often make is between probable and preferable futures. Probable futures are all those which seem *likely* to come about. They involve the projection of current trends, e.g. in relation to economic growth, unemployment or global warming, and making forecasts about what is therefore expected to happen. Preferable futures are all those which one feels *ought* to come about to achieve a particular set of value preferences. This involves envisaging, for example, what a more just and ecologically sustainable community or world might look like and the steps needed to bring it about.

Images of the future play a crucial role in the development of human life and culture. Contemporary society cannot be explained simply as the result of the *push* of the past, it is also deeply influenced by the *pull* of the future offering new and exciting possibilities. As Rick Slaughter writes:

> Images of the future present us with options and possibilities from which we can select and choose or with which we may argue and debate. Either way, they are active, shaping components of human consciousness. The main purpose of considering futures, and images of futures, is not to predict what will happen in any hard or precise sense . . . it is . . . to discern the wider ground from which images are constituted so as to take an active part both in creating and nurturing those which seem worthwhile.[9]

In the mid–1950s Fred Polak, the Dutch sociologist, wrote a major study of images of the future in Western society. He put forward the thesis that certain images of the future can develop an unusual potency and act as a societal time-bomb, creating what he called a 'breach in time.' Radically new visions of the future, he argued, can produce a sharp temporal and historical discontinuity.[10] Faced with new and potent images of the possible future society begins to mobilise its creative energies in response.

But what Polak also chronicled was that a lack of guiding images can lead to a loss of direction and purpose in society. In particular he argued that there was a decline of imaging capacity in Western society, that in the mid–20th century compelling positive images of the future were few and far between. The experiences of the First World War, the Second World War, and then the advent of the Cold War, made the future not a place of hope but one of fear. The long tradition of utopia gave way to one of anti-utopia, or dystopia, exemplified by Huxley's *Brave New World* and Orwell's *Nineteen Eighty-four.*

It is still almost impossible to watch television or go to the cinema without being faced by images of disaster, breakdown and despair. At some deep level we are haunted by these themes yet sense that something is missing. What is missing are positive guiding images of the future which can give both direction and the confidence that things *can* be radically different.

Desirable futures

What the futures field can offer is a wealth of expertise in exploring more desirable futures. It is as important to know where we *want* to get to as where we do not. As Robin Richardson comments:

> A map without utopia on it, it has been said, is not worth consulting . . . Admittedly there are disadvantages in dreams and ideals, the disadvantages of unreality and abstractions. But frequently it also clears and strengthens your mind if you venture to dream for a while, as concretely and as practically as possible, about the ideal situation to which all your current efforts are, you hope directed.[11]

This brings us back to Polak's thesis that without strong positive guiding images of the future a society loses its direction. We now need to be clear about what we *want* in the future as well as what we oppose.

Some of the most interesting work on envisioning preferable futures has been done by Warren Ziegler in the US who has worked with town planners, senior executives, hospital boards and educators and others.[12] He points out that the process takes us into often neglected areas of learning where the emphasis is on the emotional/affective and the intuitive mode, rather than the cognitive/analytic.

Elise Boulding worked with Ziegler to design and run a series of workshops on 'imaging a world without weapons'. Both had been influenced by Polak's work and concluded that 'if parties in conflict could visualise a future situation in which their conflict had been successfully managed, they would be (better) able to deal with their differences in the present in the light of that perceived future.'[13]

In describing the outcomes of such workshops Boulding notes that participants often wish to be 'realistic' and begin by assuming that their fears are realistic whilst their hopes are not. The preferable futures envisioned often share several features in common. The world described is frequently non-hierarchical, one in which a sense of locality is strong, where technology is important but low profile. Another striking image she reports is the recurrent use, especially amongst young people, of the adjectives *bright, clean,* and *green.*[14]

A quite different style of workshop, pioneered by Joanna Macy, focuses on the need first to acknowledge and then work with the feelings of pain and distress that participants experience over the state of the planet. She argues that real empowerment and action on behalf of future generations cannot occur until this deep pain is first fully experienced and shared with others.[15] This parallels the therapist's task of working with her client to express and release repressed fear and anger. When buried pain is thus unblocked creative energy becomes available for new tasks.

The utopian tradition

Every culture has its image, whether religious or secular, of a past or future better world: Eden, Arcadia, the Golden Age, Paradise. In Western thought this aspiration became known as utopia, a term coined by Thomas More in 1516 and based on a pun in Greek: 'eutopia', the good place, was also 'utopia', no place. Utopias provide blueprints for a better future society and may be presented as fiction, an ideal society set in some other time or place, or as a programme for political action and change.

Utopias always have a double-edged message: a critique of present imperfections and a vision of a better world. Literary utopias range from Plato's *Republic* to William Morris's famous *News from Nowhere* and Charlotte Gilman's *Herland*. Various groups in Europe, North America and Australia have planned and set up their own utopian communities with varying degrees of success. In Britain, for example, Gerrard Winstanley and the Diggers in the 17th century, religious groups such as the Shakers in the 18th century, and secular communities such as Robert Owen's New Harmony in the 19th.

As Krishan Kumar writes 'Utopia's value lies not in its relation to present practice but in its relation to a possible future. Its 'practical' use is to overstep the immediate reality to depict a condition whose clear desirability draws us on, like a magnet.'[16] The utopian tradition, both as literature and as lived experience, has constantly inspired critical action for change and can provide a rich source of nourishment for the creative imagination today.

Moving forwards

Other voices

We live in one world that contains many other voices telling of the future, voices that the dominant culture may often ignore. Here are four such voices.

From the Aboriginal band Yothu Yindi's album *Tribal Voice*:

> Well I heard it on the radio/ And I saw it on the television/ Back in 1988, all those talking politicians/ Words are easy, words are cheap/ Much cheaper than our priceless land/ But promises can disappear/ Just like writing in the sand/ This land was never given up/ This land was never bought and sold/ The planting of the Union Jack/ Never changed our law at all/ Now two rivers run their course/ Separated for so long/ I'm dreaming of a brighter day/ When the waters will be one[17]

Eduardo Galeano, the Uruguayan writer:

> There is just one place where yesterday and today meet, recognise each other and embrace, and that place is tomorrow. Certain voices from the American past, long past, sound very futuristic. For example, the ancient voice that still tells us we are children of the earth . . . (and) that speaks to us of community heralds another world as well. Community – the communal mode of production and life – is the oldest of American traditions . . . It belongs to the earliest days and the first people, but it also belongs to the times ahead and anticipates a New World. For there is nothing less alien to these lands of ours than socialism. Capitalism, on the other hand, is foreign: like smallpox, like the flu. It came from abroad.[18]

Vandana Shiva on women, ecology and development:

> Seen from the experience of Third World women, the modes of thinking and action that pass for science and development, respectively, are not universal and humanly inclusive, as they are made out to be; modern science and development are projects of male, western origin, both historically and ideologically . . . The industrial revolution converted economics from the prudent management of resources for sustenance and basic needs satisfaction into a process of commodity production for profit

> maximisation . . . The new relationship of man's domination and mastery over nature was thus also associated with new patterns of domination and mastery over women, and their exclusion from participation *as partners* in both science and development.[19]

And Eleonora Masini, on women as builders of the future:

> Women are better adapted for the change from the industrial society to a new society, because women are not the carriers of the values of the preceding industrial society. As they were not the builders of the future in the preceding society, they may become the builders of the future in a different society. As they were invisible in the industrial society, women may become visible and constructive in a post-industrial society.[20]

When and where in our teaching do we encourage students to listen to such voices and to draw on such traditions?

Sustainable futures

Traditional models of development and ideas of progress narrowly focus on economic growth (GNP as a measure of consumption) with its intrinsic discounting of other 'costs'. Thus some people benefit at the expense of others; people benefit at the expense of the environment; and people today benefit at the expense of future generations. Such development is not sustainable because globally more people are getting poorer, finite resources are diminishing and the environment is beginning to suffer irreversible damage. As Lester Brown comments:

> Put simply, the global economy is rigged against both poverty alleviation and environmental protection. Treating the earth's ecological ills as separate from issues of debt, trade, inequality, and consumption is like trying to treat heart disease without addressing a patient's obesity and high cholesterol diet: there is no chance of lasting success.[21]

Working towards a sustainable future requires production planned to meet human needs together with a more just distribution of resources.[22] It means reducing the harmful effects of industry and new technology, challenging company policies which are dangerous to people and the environment, stopping aid programmes which are inappropriate and damaging, reducing overconsumption and waste, restraining population growth, distinguishing clearly between wants and needs, and organising locally, nationally and internationally for appropriate change. When and where do we encourage our students to explore the need for, and nature of, sustainable development in both the local and global community?

The education we need

Educating for the future draws on two long-standing educational traditions. The first is the humanistic learner-centred tradition which focuses on the development and fulfilment of each individual. The second is concerned with building greater equality in society by challenging and transforming existing inequalities of race, gender, class and disability.[23] Each approach compliments the other and both are essential to the creation of more just and sustainable futures.

John Huckle writes:

> As the environmental problems resulting from prevailing forms of development and underdevelopment worsen, the pressure for technocentric environmental management is likely to intensify along with more calls for 'education *about* the environment.' Environmental and social educators can use the resulting opportunities to introduce elements of 'education *for* the environment' which consider the real roots of environmental issues, and allow reflection and action on genuine social and environmental alternatives. The struggle for such education in schools resembles that for more socially useful and sustainable production and development in the wider world. Both are ultimately struggles for democracy, justice and well-being, on which our future relationships with one another and with planet earth depend.[24]

This is where we need to begin, with a socially critical approach to learning that recognises the importance of changing both self and society. It requires 'the courage to admit and bear the pain of the present world', whilst at the same time 'keeping a steady eye on (our) vision of a better future.'[25]

Follow-up work

The questions raised in this chapter are ones that should be posed by all concerned with teacher education institutions. They need to be asked, and answered, by tutors about both existing and proposed courses. They are also questions which students should ask when making choices about institutions and courses.

Where and when in their education will students be encouraged to:

1. Share their feelings about the future as the third millennium approaches?
2. Learn about the crucial environmental and development issues debated at the Earth Summit in 1992?
3. Discuss the possible future impact of current global trends on their lives in the 21st century?
4. Listen to a range of different voices on the future, utopian and feminist, indigenous and non-European?
5. Explore the need for, and nature of, sustainable development both in the local and global community?
6. Ascertain how a futures perspective can be made more explicit in both National Curriculum subjects and the cross-curricular themes?

Chapter 3

PREPARING FOR THE MILLENNIUM: REFLECTIONS ON THE NEED FOR FUTURES EDUCATION

David Hicks

Teaching for a better world

If we are concerned about fully educating young people now in school for the 21st century, what sort of preparation do they need and how will the UK National Curriculum provide it? Where might explicit support for such preparation come from and what pedagogical traditions can it draw on? This chapter offers some answers to questions such as these, from the perspective of one particular UK curriculum project specifically concerned with 'education for the future'.

Section 1 of the Education Reform Act 1988 (ERA) places a statutory responsibility upon schools to provide a broad and balanced curriculum which

- promotes the spiritual, moral, cultural, mental and physical development of pupils at school and of society
- prepares pupils for the opportunities, responsibilities and experiences of adult life.[1]

Journey to the future

The personal and the professional are always inextricably intertwined, and my journey to the future is the result of many influences. It began, as for many others, in the 1950s when each Friday I avidly read of the exploits of 'Dan Dare: Pilot of the Future' in the *Eagle* comic.[2] These stories opened up speculative worlds and fascinating imaginative vistas that I had previously never dreamt of!

As a young student in the early 1960s I suffered nuclear nightmares and watched Alain Resnais's film 'Night and Fog', which showed in graphic detail life and death in the Nazi concentration camps. Later, teaching about global issues in my geography lessons seemed one important way of alerting students to the state of the planet and the need to work for a better world.

Lecturing on environmental issues at a college of education in the 1970s I was spurred on by Alvin Toffler and reading about the 'limits to growth' debate. The future seemed increasingly fascinating but hazardous and a TV documentary entitled 'Tomorrow has been cancelled due to lack of interest' only confirmed my fears.

Running a curriculum project in the 1980s gave me the opportunity to work with teachers and to develop exciting new materials on issues of global interdependence. Some teachers thought the future too abstract a concept for children to grasp. Others realized its importance and pioneered creative work with younger pupils, beginning to see the future as an important focus for concern.

Each of these critical experiences, in different ways, made me increasingly aware of the *need* for an explicit futures element in education. *How* such a concern might be introduced into the classroom was a different question. It also requires some understanding of other educational initiatives in the UK aimed at helping pupils make sense of the contemporary world.

The new utopians

A colleague was recently showing a French visitor around his institution as they discussed the state of education in the UK. 'Where,' said his guest, 'are the new utopians to be found?' 'Well actually,' responded my colleague, 'I'll be seeing them at a meeting tomorrow'. He was referring to a small group of people who were all, in different ways, involved in the promotion and practice of global education.

Global education is one of a number of terms used in the UK to highlight a range of perspectives relating to the 'state of the planet'. Most emphasize the need for a global dimension in the curriculum, based on the observation that although schools often deal with the local and the national, these can no longer be fully understood unless set in a global context.[3] We are inextricably bound up in a web of global interrelationships in which our actions and those of others can affect people and environments far distant from our own in space and time.

Most initiatives aimed at promoting a global dimension in the curriculum have come from outside the formal education system but are supported by an increasing number of teachers in both primary and secondary schools. The particular focus of such projects and programmes will vary depending on the concerns of the organization involved. Certainly all share an implicit concern for the future together with some vision of what a better world might look like.

Thus voluntary agencies such as Oxfam and Christian Aid talk about *development education*, which focuses on the North-South gap and issues of development and underdevelopment. Excellent pupil materials and support for this come from Development Education Centres such as those in Birmingham and Manchester, and others throughout the UK.[4]

Global education, or world studies, emphasizes the concept of interdependence and the need to set contemporary issues in a global context. Much good work has been done by, for example, the World Studies 8–13 Project now based at Manchester Metropolitan University[5] and the Centre for Global Education in York. During the early and mid–1980s, at the height of the Cold War, there was also considerable support for *education for peace* with its emphasis on developing skills of cooperation and conflict resolution. The Peace Pledge Union and Quaker organizations are among those which have long supported such concerns.

More recently attention has been drawn to the need for *human rights education* and its exploration of prejudice, discrimination, rights and responsibilities in a wide range of contexts. *Environmental education* is currently in vogue with the support of a wide range of organizations concerned about issues such as rainforest destruction and global warming.

Clearly many of these initiatives overlap, although each begins with a different substantive concern. One thing they share in common is the belief that, in a democratic society, young people should have the opportunity to explore a range of contemporary issues, whether to do with development, interdependence, peace and conflict, human rights, the environment, or race and gender. Ian Lister has noted these common concerns and sees the proponents of such 'new movements' as the 'vanguard educators' in social and political education.[6]

What these initiatives also have in common is an interest in the human condition and its improvement. As such, they all involve teaching for a better world and thus implicitly, if not explicity, are concerned about the future. It is to this fertile ground that we must look for any significant development of futures education in the UK. As well as being issue-oriented, these 'new movements' also share a common concern for the *process* of education, and it is this process which is at the root of effective learning.

A radical pedagogy

How young people learn is as important as *what* they learn. Most practitioners in these fields thus put great emphasis on participatory and experiential modes of learning which foster both pupil autonomy and the development of critical thinking skills. Effective learning is seen as arising out of affirmation of each pupil's individual worth, the development of a wide range of cooperative skills, the ability to discuss and debate issues, to reflect critically on everyday life and events in the wider world, and to act as responsible citizens. This requires a teaching style which is open and facilitative. Its intention is to model participation, cooperation and justice in everyday classroom interaction, believing that the medium of learning should match the message.

Such a pedagogy has been particularly well developed by those working in global education and development education, as exemplified in their in-service training for teachers, teaching materials and classroom practice.[7] This interest in, and emphasis on, process and methodology places particular emphasis on exploring the relationship between the personal and the political. It draws on two long-standing traditions in education – the person-centred tradition which emphasizes the need to develop each individual to their fullest capacity, and the reconstructionist tradition which argues that education has a crucial role to play in the betterment of society. The first focuses on the personal and thus on the wholeness of the individual, the second on the political and the wholeness of society.

One of the strengths of global education is its attempt to weave these two traditions together, a difficult but vital task, as Robin Richardson points out:

> Both traditions are concerned with wholeness and holistic thinking, but neither, arguably, is complete without the other. There cannot be wholeness in individuals independently of strenuous attempts to heal rifts and contradictions in wider society and in the education system. Conversely, political struggle to create wholeness in society – that is, equality and justice in dealings and relationships between social classes, between countries, between ethnic groups, between women and men – is doomed to no more than partial success and hollow victories, at best, if it is not accompanied by, and if it does not in its turn strengthen and sustain, the search for wholeness and integration in individuals.[8]

It has to be said that such an approach to teaching and learning is not favoured by the UK Conservative government and during the 1980s the New Right attacked proponents of global education, development education, peace education and anti-racist education. All, it was argued, involved bias and therefore the deliberate indoctrination of pupils. What they aimed to promote, however, was widespread discussion of different viewpoints on social, political and economic issues, a fundamental prerequisite for education for the future in a democratic society.

This, then, is the fertile ground in which a critical futures education can grow. It is ground which has been well prepared, both theoretically and practically, over the past decade. In particular, proponents of global education have the interest, skills and expertise that is needed to bring the futures dimension more alive in the curriculum of UK schools. If the task in the 1980s was to emphasize the need for a global dimension in the curriculum, the task of the 1990s is to highlight the need for a clear futures dimension as well.

What can the future offer?

Futures education

There is currently no distinctly recognizable field that could be called 'futures education' in the UK and, in some ways, this is probably for the best. Teachers relate much better to an expression such as education *for* the future, for this does not imply a discrete field of interest which they are not party to and which does not seem to relate to the school curriculum. In some ways, during the 1980s, teachers suffered from what might be called 'adjectival fatigue', partly brought on by the new utopians each feeling that their particular concern was paramount.

The history of an interest in education for the future in the UK is quite a short one – short in terms of explicit content, that is. Interest has tended to be implicit and from within other fields, such as global education, or has taken the form of occasional isolated units of work in school. The growth of my own interest in futures is probably fairly typical of a UK educator.

First came *Future Shock*, and then, in 1972, *The Limits to Growth*, ideas from which I enthusiastically incorporated into my geography and humanities teaching at school. Subsequently Toffler's *Learning for Tomorrow* gave a much firmer pedagogical base to these interests. Later, when lecturing at a college of education, I was most excited by an Open University unit on *Designing the Future* which I used in my work on environmental issues with student teachers.[9] By the end of the 1970s the future was very much on my agenda.

When the World Studies 8–13 curriculum project was set up in 1980 we wanted to include within it a specific focus on alternative futures. The purpose of this project was to run in-service courses for teachers at both primary and secondary level and to develop practical resources which would help children in the 8–13 age range explore issues of global interdependence.[10] Much of our inspiration of the futures element came from the excellent National Council for the Social Studies publication *Futures Unlimited: Teaching About Worlds to Come*, which seemed a synthesis of much of the best work coming from the USA.[11]

At the same time Rick Slaughter was beginning his research on critical futures studies at the University of Lancaster. Liaison with Rick during this period provided a steady flow of ideas relating to the possibilities inherent in future studies.[12] The Project's first resource book for teachers appeared in 1985 and included a chapter called 'The world tomorrow'. This contained a range of practical classroom activities for exploring the future with younger pupils.[13]

A lecture tour in Australia brought the work of Noel Gough to my attention, initially through his contribution to the volume *Teaching Geography for a Better World*. This text epitomizes the valuable work that can be done to address issues of current and future global concern via a specific discipline.[14] It shows with great clarity how insights from political education, environmental education, multicultural education, women's studies and futures education, can be incorporated into the mainstream secondary curriculum. Similar volumes from other subject specialists would be most welcome.

In particular I found Noel's work on the conceptualization of futures in educational discourse valuable. He thus identifies three types of reference to the future – 'tacit, token and taken for granted'.[15] 'Tacit futures' are those which are assumed and never brought out into the open. They remain hidden and unexplicated but nevertheless present. Thus the future may not even be mentioned in an educational document but assumptions about it are still tacitly present. 'Token futures' often involve clichés and stereotypes presented in a rhetorical fashion. Gough notes, 'When one finds "the future" (or a futures-oriented inference) in the title of an educational document it usually means much less than might be expected'. 'Taken-for-granted futures' occur whenever a particular future, or range of futures, is described as if there were no other alternatives. Discussion of the future framed solely in terms of science and technology or work and leisure would be in this category.

In beginning a new curriculum project on alternative futures I have thus drawn on, and been inspired by, initiatives such as these. In searching for UK examples of resource materials for teachers, however, the trail runs thin. The main sources of explicit classroom activities on futures are sections in Fisher and Hicks, *World Studies 8–13: A Teacher's Handbook*, and Pike and Selby, *Global Teacher, Global Learner*.[16]

Shorter, but important, sources by Slaughter are found in *Education for Peace: Issues, Principles and Practice in the Classroom*, and by Gough in *Teaching Geography for a Better World*.[17] Although booklets like Slaughter's *Futures Tools and Techniques* and *Studying the Future*[18] are also invaluable, such Australian sources are not readily available to teachers in the UK. The same goes for US materials such as *Future Images: Future Studies for Grades 4 to 12* by Whaley.[19] A lot of other teaching materials, especially in global education and environmental education, have a strong futures orientation but are not directly about futures *per se*.

Alternative futures

The second source of my inspiration for developing futures education is the work of academics, researchers and others specifically working in the futures field. During the early 1980s I designed and taught a unit for a BA degree in Social Ethics called 'War, peace and the future' and, in preparing for this, had to identify useful texts for students.

I found Beres and Targ's *Constructing Alternative World Futures* particularly useful, especially the chapters on 'Normative theory, alternative futures and academic discourse' and 'The utopian and anarchist traditions as alternative world futures'[20] These gave, respectively, a conceptual framework for sources of ideas about alternative world futures, and a reminder of the long-standing historical traditions to which the field is related. Similarly, Freeman and Jahoda's *World Futures: The Great Debate*, explored a range of worldviews and scenarios, focusing in particular on the differences between conservative, reformist and radical perspectives.[21] Further explication of high growth/low growth and inegalitarian/more equal scenarios, applied to a range of issues, offered a diversity of alternative futures on which to reflect.

A smaller work, which popularized these concerns, was Robertson's *The Sane Alternative: A Choice of Futures*[22] This described five future scenarios: business as usual; disaster; authoritarian control; hyper-expansionist; and sane, humane, ecological. Much of the book is taken up with elaboration of the last scenario as the only one which is a sufficient response to current global crises. Students found this one of the most readable texts and it is still one that I recommend to teachers.

On preparing to set up the Global Futures Project in 1989 I looked again to see what writing by futurists might be of use in my work with teachers. They ranged from the sublime to the ridiculous. In the former category is Marien and Jenning's *What I have Learned: Thinking About the Future Then and Now*[23] This contains some of the best critically reflective writing on futures, particularly the chapters by Wagar, Harman, Ferkiss, Michael, Dator and Henderson. Their insights are a joy to return to and a constant source of inspiration.

In the latter category, however, is Coates and Jarratt's *What Futurists Believe*[24] This is saved from being unbelievably awful by contributions from people such as Boulding and Marien, and the chapter on 'Strengths, weaknesses and gaps in current futures thinking'. The latter notes that contributors generally lack vision, work to keep their ethical principles invisible, focus on problems rather than opportunities, do not include women, minorities or everyday concerns in their views and generally fail to examine their assumptions! Maybe this is because the futurists they selected generally operate on taken-for-granted, western, male, corporate views of the future.

As we enter the last decade of the 20th century, and the millennium approaches, I suspect that we will be greeted by a plethora of books about the future. Many of these may be ones that teachers and older pupils will pick up and read. Their uncritical 'pop-futurist' nature may well militate against the more considered views that futures education would wish to encourage. Three recent examples are Naisbitt and Aburdene's *Megatrends 2000*, Kinsman's *Millennium*, and Toffler's *Powershift*.[25]

Although the 'millennial megatrends' described by Naisbitt and Aburdene are all clearly of interest, it is, by and large, a very North American view of the world. Little attention is paid to the hopes and fears of the marginalized and dispossessed. Indeed, little attention is really paid to two-thirds of the world's population, except in as much as they partake of a 'global', ie consumer-orientated, 'lifestyle'. This really is a rich-world view of the future.

Kinsman's book is interesting in that it focuses on changes in the business world. He also describes in some detail the Taylor Nelson/Applied Futures seven social value groups, which are then aggregated into inner-directed, outer-directed and sustenance-driven groups. Depending on which of these social groups comes to prevail, three alternative scenarios for the UK over the next 30 years are given: 'Caring autonomy', 'Assertive materialism' and 'Retrenchment'. Like all scenarios they represent an over-simplification of reality, but are interesting materials for debate and discussion.

Toffler's latest book on global power shifts, with its arcane chapter headings, feels highly indigestible. It is too long and too wordy, a morass of uncritical assertions. I also have problems with anyone who says that the North-South gap is now fading. It is far too easy for the rich to write off the poor.

A critical global education, or futures education, requires that we recognize and confront ethical dilemmas, rather than just describe them. In doing so we need to listen to the voices of those who suffer injustice, which is still the majority of inhabitants on this planet.

Preparing for the millennium

The Global Futures Project

This curriculum project is the first of its kind in the UK specifically to promote the need for a futures dimension in the school curriculum. It draws much of its strength and support from 'vanguard educators' working in global education and allied fields. Like many such projects it is a modest venture externally financed, in this case initially by the Worldwide Fund for Nature UK.

In particular, the project aims to help teachers and pupils:

- develop a more *future-orientated* perspective both on their own lives and events in the wider world;
- identify and envision *alternative futures* which are just and sustainable;

- exercise *critical thinking* skills and the *creative imagination* more effectively;
- participate in more thoughtful and informed *decision making* in the present;
- engage in active and *responsible citizenship*, both in the local, national and global community, and on behalf of present and future generations.

It is hoped that the project will have a wide application. It should be of interest to primary and secondary teachers concerned with subjects such as English, maths, science, technology, geography, history, modern languages, and religious education. It is also of particular relevance to equal opportunities, multicultural education, and cross-curricular themes such as environmental education, citizenship, economic understanding and careers.

Six project themes have been identified which will form the basis for pupil and teacher materials as well as in-service work (Table 1).

Table 1. Project themes

Where are we now? (The situation)

(1) Thinking about the future

Pupils share their thoughts about the future, about change and about time. They then use these ideas to reassess their current interests and concerns, in relation to their personal lives, the local community and the wider world.

(2) Probable futures

Next pupils clarify how they expect the future to be. What different futures do they anticipate for themselves and for the world? What images do others have of such probable futures?

Where do we want to get to? (The vision)

(3) Preferable futures

Pupils identify their own preferred futures and compare them with those of others. In particular they will be encouraged to explore what just and ecologically sustainable futures might look like, both globally and in their own daily lives.

(4) The Utopian tradition
Pupils study ways in which people in the past have tried to put their visions of the 'good society' into practice. By exploring life in selected utopian communities pupils further clarify their own values and priorities for the future.

How do we get there? (Action)
(5) Projects for change
Pupils then re-focus on the present by investigating the work of groups and organizations committed to creating critical social change, eg in relation to justice, the environment, equal opportunities and development issues.

(6) Active citizenship
Pupils then plan and carry out their own projects for change at home, in school and the local community. In so doing they learn to match future local/global needs with socially critical and ecologically responsible citizenship today.

The project has recently produced *Educating for the Future: A Practical Classroom Guide*. This takes an issue-based approach to teaching and learning and is intended to enhance ongoing work in the National Curriculum. It is primarily for use with pupils in the 9–14 age group.[26]

Work in progress

The project is still in its early stages and is in the process of identifying interested schools and teachers to work with. However, teachers are currently preoccupied with implementing the new UK National Curriculum. Both school and Local Education Authority funding is also in short supply, so teachers cannot easily get out of school to go on in-service courses. On occasions when this *is* possible, however, and the practical significance of education for the future can be experienced, considerable enthusiasm generally follows.

Children are always immediately interested in the future as these quotations from 10-year-olds in a Berkshire school indicate:

- 'I hope that in the future there will be no more war and hunger and the world will become green and everybody will care to make it better and the world will unite again.'

- 'My hopes for the future are to have a happy life and to live for a long time and have a nice family. And that my cat and goldfish will live for a long time. . . .'
- 'One of my fears for the future is that I'll get hijacked in a 'plane, another is that I'll get stuck in an elevator.'
- 'Another world fear is that the atmosphere will get too polluted so that we cannot live any longer.'

Concerns range from the personal to the global, from families and pets to the welfare of other people and the planet itself.

One way of beginning work on futures with pupils is to encourage them to ask 'Questions about the future'. This activity permits them to formulate their *own* questions about the future and the teacher to identify the particular interests of the class. The procedure is as follows:

- Each child writes down individually five questions she/he would like to ask about the future. There is no limitation as to their scope. They may be personal, about school, the local community, or events in the wider world.
- Children then work in groups of five or six to put similar questions together and then rank them by popularity. Each group can thus identify their 'top 10' questions.
- Alternatively, the aim can be to arrive at a list of top 10 questions for the class as a whole. One such list eventually agreed upon by a class of seven-year-olds in Taunton is shown on Table 2.

Table 2. Questions about the future

Will I still be laughing when I'm 50?
Will we find out about Pluto?
Will our friends be the same?
What will our mums and dads look like?
Will there be a war soon?
How many more animals will be extinct?
Will the jungles be destroyed?
Will cars still have leaded petrol?
Will pollution stop divers going under the sea?
Will people still use pencils?
Will they invent irons to run off solar heat?

Year 3, Blackbrook School, Taunton (January 1991).

- Children then work in pairs to discuss and research possible answers to their questions using resource books in class or in the library and/or by interviewing other people in school or at home. Of course, in many cases they will find that there is no agreed 'right' answer and thus begin to learn about the need to tolerate ambiguity and differences of opinion.
- Finally each pair presents to the class in written, visual or spoken form the results of their research and/or interviews.

The project Interim Guide contained within it a range of embryonic ideas, all of which need further development, both for use as part of in-service work with teachers and with students in the classroom. Six in particular are briefly noted here. Each has a critical role to play in the development of futures education in the 1990s.

Views of the future

Students need to understand that people's hopes and fears for the future vary enormously depending, among other things, on age, gender, race and class. These differences urgently require further investigation. Any notion of a just world order requires that we ask, '*Whose* future are we talking about?', 'Who will benefit/lose from such a scenario?'[27]

Feminist perspectives

Some of the most important insights into preferred futures come from feminist writers, whether this is in relation to development issues, ecofeminism, or women's utopias. These perspectives are crucial to any understanding of the present and how it has been shaped by patriarchy. Attention needs to be paid, therefore, to how such insights can be used to challenge and transform current educational practice.[28]

Intergenerational justice

Notions of justice are now being expanded by philosophers, lawyers and economists to include the rights of future generations. Justice is thus seen as having both a spatial and a temporal dimension. How do we help students develop a sense of responsibility towards future generations? How do we help students ensure that the next generation inherits no less natural and manufactured wealth than we ourselves?[29]

Envisioning the future. Images of the future are a crucial element in the creation of change. They play a powerful role in what students think is, or is not, worth doing. Envisioning preferable futures needs to be a vital part of futures education and much more common in educational practice generally. This needs to acknowledge both our pain for what is happening to this planet and its peoples and also our visions of more just and sustainable futures.[30]

Sustainability. One of the most important concepts for students to understand and explore is the notion of sustainable development. This emphasizes the need to meet the needs of the least advantaged in society, without causing further undue environmental damage and also taking into account the needs of future generations. Students need to understand what sustainability looks like at home, in school and in the local community, and be prepared to commit themselves to its furtherance.[31]

Utopian traditions. There is a long utopian tradition in western thought which focuses on the nature of the good life and the perfect society. Utopians may present their ideas as fiction, where the ideal society is set in some other time or place, or as a programme for political action, or in the form of intentional communities. This living tradition has much to offer students and others interested in exploring preferable futures.[32]

Epilogue

Although the current educational climate in the UK may seem unsupportive for new initiatives from 'vanguard educators', the times demand that innovation in fields such as futures education continues. The state of the planet as we approach the third millennium *is* a perilous one. Our unique capacity for imagining alternative futures urgently needs to be revitalized and used compassionately in the transformation of the planet.

> The utopian imagination, at its most radical, invades the prevailing concept of reality, undermines certainties about what humans must always be like, and casts doubts upon the inevitabilities of the relations of everyday life.[33]

One hundred years ago, in the 1890s, the great designer, writer and activist, William Morris, struggled with his socialist comrades to create a better world – one which, in part, we have now inherited. He well recognized the complexities of that struggle.

> I pondered how men [*sic*] fight and lose the battle, and the thing they fought for comes about in spite of their defeat, and when it comes turns out not to be what they meant, and other men have to fight for what they meant under another name.[34]

Yet the only thing we can influence by our actions is the future. To transform the world and the structures of our own lives are ultimately one and the same.

Follow-up work

The questions arising from Chapter 3 focus on students' own interests in the future and the ways in which such concerns can be articulated in the curriculum for the 1990s. It is useful to identify in advance what books are available in the library that deal in any way with alternative futures.

1. David Hicks describes some of the influences that have contributed to his own interest in the future. What are some of the influences – events, people, books – that have helped form *your* own views of the future? How do these affect your approach to your chosen field of study?
2. Ian Lister's 'vanguard educators' have played an important role in keeping contemporary global issues on the educational agenda. Either contact one of the addresses cited for further information or write a review of one of the resources mentioned in the text. (See references page 120.)
3. David Hicks suggests that as we approach the millennium publications and articles about the future will become more common. Can you find any evidence to support this? Keep an eye on television programmes, newstands and in bookshops. What views of the future are being offered?
4. Try out the activity called 'Questions about the future' which is described on page 34. How similar or different are the chosen questions to those shown in Table 2? What might some of the reasons be for such similarities/differences?

5. Where and how in your particular subject or field of interest can you make exploration of alternative futures a more explicit part of the curriculum?

Chapter 4

CHANGING IMAGES OF FUTURES IN THE 20TH CENTURY

Richard A. Slaughter

Futures, and images of futures, play a much greater part in our lives and culture than is commonly realized. Far from being distant abstractions, futures concerns in general are constitutive of our common humanity. Without a forward-looking temporal context we could not create plans, purposes, goals, intentions . . . or meanings. Human life and culture cannot be described or explained simply by referring to the *push* of the past. It is also profoundly influenced by the *pull* of the future. Sir Karl Popper, scourge of historicism, put the point very clearly:

> the open future is, almost as a promise, as a temptation, as a lure, present; indeed actively present, at every moment. The old world picture that puts before us a mechanism operating with causes that are all in the past – the past kicking and driving us

> with kicks into the future – the past that is gone is no longer adequate to our indeterministic world . . . It is not the kicks from the back, from the past, that impel us, but the attraction, the lure of the future and its attractive possibilities that entice us: this is what keeps life – and, indeed, the world – unfolding.[1]

Images of the future present us with options and possibilities from which we can select and choose or with which we may argue and debate. Either way, they are active, shaping components of human consciousness. The main purpose of considering futures, and images of futures, is not to predict what will happen in any hard or precise sense, nor even to select from alternatives. It is, perhaps, to discern *the wider ground from which images are constituted* so as to take an active part both in creating and nurturing those which seem worthwhile.

The literature on imaging futures is limited, and some is superficial. Academic treatments are useful in sketching in the research background, but they may overlook wider cultural concerns.[2] In this chapter I look at more promising sources and consider the human and cultural significance of imaging.

Imaging as a social process

Imaging is by no means a specialized or impersonal activity. It plays a central guiding role in many creative vocations. Consider the writer. He or she may well begin with just one central image. If the image is a compelling one it acts like a magnet and, over time, draws towards it the other details from which a story can be woven – context, characters, plot and so on. Similarly, an architect or an interior designer is likely to begin a new project with a series of sketches or 'roughs'. These evolve into detailed blueprints and plans. The artist or sculptor often works in the same fundamental way: first comes the concept or image; next the process of refining it; finally there is the hard work of translating images and concepts into a finished product. Social imaging seems to conform to this general pattern.

Imaging is a social process with a long history. If we consider some of the major works of antiquity – the Parthenon, the pyramids, the Great Wall of China – it is evident that they would never have been built without a strong guiding image. The stupendous labour involved could not have been undertaken if this image had not been capable of marshalling a powerful social effort to turn an 'image-ined' reality into a real and tangible one. So, at the social level, the right image can act as a cultural force to bring new projects to fruition.

Such images may be visual or they may be more abstractly symbolic. Consider Martin Luther King's 'I have a dream . . .' speech. Or John Kennedy's 'We choose to go to the moon . . .'. Both helped to define and focus a collective effort to realize major social goals: in one case social justice for black people in the USA; in the other a largely technical effort to realize culturally significant goals (self-confidence, leadership over the Soviets). However, grand visions have become relatively rare in the 20th century. Why is this?

One reason is that contemporary views of futures tend to be not so much about the things we want to achieve as about the things we want to avoid – pollution, the greenhouse effect, the loss of tropical forests. Outside engineering contexts, it is hard to find grand visions to compare with those which provided coherence and direction in other cultures at other times. The late 20th century equivalents of the Great Exhibition (held in London at the Crystal Palace in 1851) manifestly do not represent the triumphant expression of a clearly expressed vision, so much as a desperate, even manic, attempt at reassurance. Behind the slick technology and laser light shows, there is a seldom acknowledged *lack* of confidence and vision.[3] That, perhaps, is why occasions such as the Brisbane Expo draw much more heavily on the mass entertainment values of Disneyland than the assured and optimistic cultural values such as were expressed and displayed at the Crystal Palace. But then, this is a very different age.

The contrast between expo as escapism and expo as confident statement is fairly stark. It expresses a major shift in our views of the world – and the future – during the present century.

Beyond utopia and dystopia

The attempt to imagine ideal societies has a long and honourable past. For over 400 years writers, scholars and speculators of many different persuasions put pen to paper and tried to imagine how the ills of their societies could be overcome and new possibilities created. From Sir Thomas More's classic *Utopia* (1516) onwards there was a vast and varied outpouring of such material. It prepared the ground for many social innovations which we now take for granted – health insurance, democratic government, courts of law and the emancipation of women, to mention only a few.

Perhaps the last great utopia was H. G. Wells's attempt to write what he called *A Modern Utopia* (1905). It was a bold vision based on the assumed benefits of science and technology. But there was also a darker side to the picture. Wells not only saw the rational organization of human affairs leading to an era of peace and prosperity. He also foresaw the armoured land tank and nuclear weapons. There is a powerful description of the latter in one of his later books. He worried endlessly about what he termed 'human folly'.

Four years after the publication of Wells's utopia, another writer produced a powerful story which considered the dark side of Wells's vision. The writer in question was E. M. Forster and his story was called *The Machine Stops*. It was, and remains, a powerful vision of a world in which all human life is dependent on machines. It is a repressive, high-tech future in which people have forgotten how to control 'the machine' and have also forgotten that technology takes away even as it provides.[4]

So at the beginning of the 20th century we see the long tradition of utopia giving way to anti-utopia (or dystopia). The twin extremes represent two poles of our destiny – progress and disaster. The interesting thing is that as the present century has passed, so it has become progressively *easier* to imagine dystopia and *harder* to believe in progress. Utopia has even been subjected to negative reversals which suggest that notions of social improvement are 'unrealistic', pie-in-the-sky or oppressively overbearing. There have certainly been many dystopian images and events to draw on – overcrowded cities, polluted seas, dying animals and birds, stark images of famine, war and decay. The use of nuclear weapons at the end of World War II, the growing fears for the environment and a pervasive sense of uncertainty and loss of control have made the future appear increasingly problematic. The implications are far from obvious because the impacts of such shifts frequently take place in hidden, unregarded ways. After noting that people can be regarded as symbolic animals who seek meaning, Dunphy notes that 'it is at the symbolic level that change hits us hardest, because it so frequently tears apart symbols which have provided our lives with meaning and continuity'.[5]

In popular culture we have become so accustomed to moods of cynicism, violence and despair that it may not be immediately obvious how inhibiting they can be. The great dystopias of the century (Huxley's *Brave New World* and Orwell's *Nineteen Eighty-four*) clearly articulated widely felt concerns about depersonalization and other threats to our well-being. So far, so good. But they are succeeded by entire industries which now permeate the global village. In the 1990s it is almost impossible to contemplate an evening's television viewing or the week's films without noting references back to familiar dystopian themes of disaster, decay and dissolution. Clearly our preoccupation with bright and new technologies has not fooled the collective unconscious: something important is missing. This sense of loss is faithfully reproduced in the mass media. Yet they reveal little awareness either of the proliferation of negative futures imagery or of the human implications of ersatz surrogate worlds. A number of observers have commented on how the latter misrepresent social reality in important ways.[6] In other words, the distortions of the technological screen between us and the natural world complicate the task of understanding it and of acting to preserve it for future generations.

It is not that dystopia is necessarily 'bad' in any simple-minded way. The great dystopias can also be read as warnings, destinations to avoid. As components on a map of futures, areas of danger are as important as possible destinations. Moreover, the subjects of such warnings can be falsified by concerted action. Such is the power of applied foresight. On the other hand, anodyne or apparently positive images may conceal many dangers behind a seemingly harmless facade. This should alert us to the fact that, like optimism and pessimism, utopia and dystopia are ambiguous. Care should be taken in believing and interpreting them. These simple oppositions have more to do with the preference of the human mind for polar contrasts than with a profoundly interconnected world. The latter demands a deeper approach to the imaging dilemma.

Responding to the imaging dilemma

As we near the end of the 20th century there is an inevitable growth of interest in the year 2000 and the new millennium. Such transitions are much more than artefacts of a numbering system; they have enormous cultural significance. Hence, projects to celebrate the historical divide are already being conceived. But, at the same time, this is taking place in a context in which compelling images of futures are few and far between. It might appear that our long-term social imaging capacity is failing at the very time when it is needed most. Yet this is partly a question of perspective. It turns on the fact that we already live in a period which incorporates many features that earlier generations thought of as being 'in the future'. Men have walked on the moon. Human hearts are routinely transplanted. We can speak to each other across the entire world and photograph distant planets. But the *technical* achievements of yesterday soon lose their power to uplift and inspire. Perhaps we should reflect on this hint that today's marvels may not be all they are advertised to be.

Two contradictory factors can be observed. On the one hand, there has been a loss of confidence about our ability to solve major problems and to survive in a world severely compromised by human activity. On the other hand, we have already achieved many things which people worked towards when they were only dreams and visions located 'in the future'. We live longer, travel further, and know more than ever before. But the social capacity to imagine new and different futures has clearly declined. What can we do about this? There are a number of options.

First, we can recognize that this apparent exhaustion of imaging capacity is only temporary. The human and cultural *sources* of images have certainly not been lost. In some ways they are stronger and more accessible than ever before (see below). While many have been relegated to the cultural margins, they can be reclaimed and utilized. Second, we can revalue countertraditions that incorporate visionary elements which breach the bounds of everyday assumptions and practices.[7] Third, it is entirely reasonable to suggest that a great deal more effort be devoted to scanning and exploring futures. But to achieve this will necessitate a fundamental shift of perception. This shift is primarily one which revalues the future; which sees it not as an abstraction or an empty space but as a principle of present action.

Futures people do need to be clear about what they do. They need to explain clearly, and in many different contexts, how it is that the full implications of many actions, policies or decisions made in the present cannot be understood or explained without considering a wide range of future implications. In this view foresight and futures study may well need to take precedence over studies of the past. I do not see this as asserting a false opposition between historians and futurists, for these are complementary enterprises. But this is far from being merely an academic issue. It is important to initiate the kinds of social processes whereby people are encouraged to participate in imagining the kinds of futures they would like to live in and pass on to their children. Such processes are not particularly easy to create and sustain. But we certainly know enough to make a good start. A culture which can invent wonder drugs and place machines in orbit should not shrink from such work simply because it is human and cultural, rather than scientific and technical. That very partiality (towards the assumed dominance of science and technology) is itself a longstanding continuity which frames our present dilemma.

So while pessimism certainly seems uppermost, there are grounds for reestablishing more constructive views. Those grounds can be explored and developed almost without limit. They can be likened to a set of tools waiting to be taken up, elaborated and used more widely. To be more specific, both 'positive' and 'negative' images can be critiqued. Futures workshops can help people to establish different images and use them as 'magnets' for personal goals or social innovations of many kinds. Nor need the directives and imperatives set by technology fads and international capital be passively followed. Other alternatives can be consciously cultivated.

Among the most penetrating options available is our ability to probe beneath the surface of the industrial worldview, discern its systemic defects and renegotiate some deeply embedded assumptions and values.[8] This may mean adopting and implementing a stewardship ethic, attending to the rights of future generations, or redefining growth. There is no shortage of important, socially responsible work to be done in such areas. Quite the contrary, if we cannot reinvent the culture and its worldview the prophets of doom will be proved right. Finally, there is value in looking for a different historical dynamic – perhaps one which owes less to a machine-led view of the world and more to an informed, even visionary, view of human development. Since each of these involves imaging processes, the remainder of this article considers them in more detail.

Critique of futures images

Images of futures are constantly being produced, consumed, applied and discarded. At any particular time certain images are gathering social support or losing it. While, in practice, too little critical attention is given to them, all such images can be renegotiated, reconceptualized, refashioned or refused. Take the example of images of futures in young people's media.

A survey I carried out not long ago suggested that, in this context, 'the future' was primarily constituted of powerful machines, technologies, space rockets and robots.[9] But credible views of future people *as people* (not as props for the surrounding technosphere) were almost entirely absent. More odd still was that much of the material exhibited confusions in some important areas – good and evil, right and wrong, science and magic seemed interchangeable or incoherent. Even on the level of such simple contrasts, it seemed to me that inversions and category errors here could not but work *against* the child's attempts to construct a coherent picture of the world and his/her role in it. There is clearly a long way to go before children's media adequately portray the range and symbolic richness of futures images or seriously explore alternative, non-standard views. On the other hand this very lack suggests opportunities for a wealth of original work.

Such tendencies are not restricted to children's media. Technophilia is a dominant characteristic of popular television programmes which explore 'recent developments in science and technology'. They come very close to assuming that the future will actually be built largely of machines which can be photographed and presented in short punchy sequences by young reporters. The resulting images are little other than pure entertainment. Such programmes mystify the public by suggesting that 'the future' can be assimilated to such limited concerns, by their ignorance of the social relations of science and technology and by their habit of entirely overlooking the rich web of concepts and imagery which could provide a broader picture.[10]

Another source of futures imagery is associated with science fiction (SF) literature and film. Limitations of space preclude in-depth analysis. Sufficient to say that one purpose of speculative artwork is to dramatize events taken from the plots of SF books and to situate them visually in a variety of different worlds – past, present and future. Much of the imagery – particularly from the pulp era, pre–1950 – is fairly crude. Yet even then artists such as Virgil Findlay and Frank Hampson produced high-quality images which still stand up today.[11] From this more accomplished tradition, people like Roger Dean, Giger (designer of 'Alien') and Sorayama have emerged with a varied body of material which provides a variety of images of futures. Since these may impact on wider imaging processes, they can legitimately be subjected to criticism.

For example, Sorayama has produced a series of 'sexy robots' – impossibly feminine machines in bright, curving steel. On one level he is simply playing with us: 'gaze on this steel perfection and all you'll see is your own reflection. There's not a spark of life, not a single breath of individuality in these chrome bodies . . .'.[12] On another level he has tapped two converging streams of mythology, the perfect body and the perfect machine. They make a compelling – if repellant – combination. Both are fantasies, but fantasies supported by the prevalent myths of the age. A related fantasy, and perhaps a more dangerous one, is that of the 'humanized' robot – the robot with the child on its knee, the robot which 'sleeps'. There is one particularly striking image on the cover of an Asimov novel which portrays a robot 'resting'. It is a seductive image done in pastel colours, conveying repose. How should we respond? Should we agree so readily that *human* qualities and capacities may simply be read on machines? It seems unwise. While, in fact, the *physical* boundaries between people and machines are being progressively breached, it is important to resist the dehumanization which could follow. Images which forge ahead into this transition without comment could be the thin edge of a dangerous wedge.

Two other types of futures imagery can be briefly mentioned here. One is the growth of engineering futures imagery, particularly in Japan. There the Taisei Corporation has embarked on an ambitious design and PR programme to popularize its notion of 'Alice cities' (after Alice in Wonderland). The images are spectacular – vast underground cityscapes, remote buried factories, immense crystal domes and so on. One widely reproduced image shows a perspective cut-away of a cylindrical underground structure with ramps, walkways, numerous levels and, of course, a swimming pool. A wooded landscape stretches away towards another forest of immense tower blocks. It is an heroic image. Considerable efforts have been expended on the detailed visualization of the project. A letter from the deputy general manager states, in part: 'Thank you for paying attention to our Alice cities. We believe our ideas will come true in the 21st century. However, we have to clear so many hurdles to implement them. We really need the support of many people . . .'.[13]

This is a fine example of futures imagery deployed as part of a wider strategy. However, it is important to use such images *as a starting point* for looking deeper. While the Taisei drawings 'probe beneath the surface' in a physical sense, there is no evidence of a comparable effort to uncover ideological or epistemological questions. In some ways the latter is the more important task, yet it may not be an easy one to pursue in a corporate context where strategic directions may be unquestioned and, indeed, unquestionable. Given certain assumptions Alice cities could represent a real option for a land- and resource-poor country. Yet with different assumptions they could become a technocratic nightmare.

Early images of futures also have their uses. As I. F. Clarke and others have shown, such images played an important part in the attempt to speculate about times to come.[14] But, with the benefit of hindsight, they can be used to gain a different perspective on our own time. For example a set of cigarette cards called 'En l'an 2000' were produced by French illustrator Jean Marc Cote in 1899, but were never used. They were re-discovered many years later and published as *Future Days*.[15] The images show personal helicopters, pranks under the sea and numerous applications of mechanical lever technology – for example in farming, tailoring and even shaving!

It is almost instinctual to look for where the artist 'got it wrong'. But it is more useful to consider that, just as he worked with the assumptions of his own time, so, 100 years later, do we. When we look ahead we virtually ignore lever technology. Instead we appear to believe that computers and information will predominate. So we populate our images and thoughts of futures with them. But what if they turn out to be radically limited in certain important ways? Perhaps they will look as silly in 100 years as the mechanical barber does now. We may be sure that in another century some of the things we believe will also turn out to be false or trivial. But it is in the nature of things that we cannot know what they are. In other words past images of futures comment on historical contingency and therefore provide grounds for caution.

Futures workshops

Futures workshops provide a flexible way of dealing with futures concerns, nurturing images, and exploring their implications in a small group context. Some workshops are exploratory and open-ended, some are more highly structured. Some combine both approaches. Among the most highly structured are those pioneered by Boulding and Ziegler. Similar in philosophy, but not in approach, are those developed over a number of years by Robert Jungk.[16] There are a number of distinct phases, as illustrated in Table 1.

These workshops can be run in a day, a weekend or longer. They deliberately intertwine rational – logical and intuitive – emotional strands. They are intended to provide fora in which people can reflect on issues of concern to them and from there produce a plan for action which may result in a social innovation or other creative change. They have been held in a number of European countries with evident success.

Table 1. Outline of Robert Jungk's Futures Workshops

Preparation
Announcement of themes, place, time, cost etc. Meeting place, seating, facilities. Materials. Opening: introduction, workshop structure and procedures, timetable, introductions.

Critique
State the problem, log key points and choose key ones. Form clusters and amalgamate key points. Pick clusters or statement by voting.

Fantasy
Objectives – re-write selected key points or statements in positive form. Warmup via playing fantasy games. Brainstorming to gather ideas. Choose ideas with the greatest potential. Fantasy clusters. Collect related items together into clusters. Form small groups to work up into 'Utopian schemes'.

Implementation
Display results so far. Choose the most popular ideas to take further. Check selections for practicability. Try to foresee difficulties. Choose a project and develop an action plan.

Continuation
Extend earlier workshop material via brainstorming and amplification. Outline options and select one by voting. Review feasibility and finalize objectives. Implement plan and evaluate performance.

A different approach is to use a guided fantasy to elicit images of futures. Noel Wilson of South Australia uses this method with teenagers in Australia and the UK. He works from a prepared script to take the participants through several stages. First, there is a relaxation stage. Next, they are taken on a journey into the clouds. Finally they return to earth in some future time and draw what they see. From numerous examples, Wilson was able to draw a clear composite picture. He wrote:

> some six hundred students later, a clear pattern had emerged. Over half of the scenarios were dominated by computers and robots housed in block houses, skyscrapers, and ubiquitous domes. Over half contained landscapes of bleak devastation. Nearly all were negative and dehumanised. Most were devoid of humans.[17]

It is clear from this work and that of many others that young people tend to have very negative views of their likely futures.[18] The question is, how can teachers and others help them to move away from the pain and anguish involved and explore other options? Are there ways of moving out of the depression and learning to *respond* to the fears? I believe that there are.

Resources for dealing with fears

Joanna Macy is a leading practitioner in this area. Her *Despair and Personal Power in the Nuclear Age*[19] offers a rich compendium of strategies which deal directly with feelings of helplessness, anger, grief and so on. She articulates five principles:

1 Feelings of pain for our world are natural and healthy.
2 This pain is morbid only if denied.
3 Information alone is not enough.
4 Unblocking repressed feelings releases energy, clears the mind.
5 Unblocking our pain for the world reconnects us with the larger web of life.

Much of her work takes place in workshops and retreats in locations around the world. These workshops can be powerful since they elicit human responses at fairly profound levels. This occurs not simply because of her grasp of group processes, but, more important, because she herself has explored some of the richest grounds for cultural innovation and the recovery of meaning. She is a practising Buddhist and draws on this (and other traditions) for insight and understanding. Hence, Macy's workshops are based on more than technique. They are founded on a deep understanding of the human predicament, on a substantial involvement with the theory and practice of deep ecology and on a vision of an interconnected and indivisible world. The vision is embodied in various ways – in Eastern and shamanic symbolism, in deep ecology ritual and in the re-spiritualization of experience. The tenor of this approach may best be gauged from her teaching at an intensive seminar in northern England, where she declared:

> It sometimes seems that all that can save us is a miracle. However, from a deep ecology viewpoint we *are* a miracle. The work is very much about attending upon a miracle. It does not have to do with our doing. That is where the smile (ie of the Buddha) comes in. The connections do not need to be made. They are there. The web is not an idea. It is a reality. Peace is not something you make. It is the dance of our true selves. It is the thrust of life which has woven itself through rocks, through waters, through times, travels and forms we cannot imagine.[20]

Such an approach must be deployed with care and sensitivity. Yet when it is done well it has the effect of reframing issues and concerns and then *linking* the human response to powerful cultural resources at the levels necessary for insights and resolutions to occur. This can be seen in the Council of all Beings, a deeply moving ritual in which people identify closely with different creatures or features of the environment and speak as if from that perspective.[21] With this in mind, two further principles can be outlined:

1 The critical factor in dealing with fears is *the nature of the human response* to the situation(s) from which the fears derive. A group context means that a wider range of potential responses is available.
2 The resources deployed to deal with fears must be adequate to the task and will therefore tend to be grounded primarily in cultural and spiritual traditions, and only secondarily in technique or psychology. This helps to explain why more instrumental, goal-oriented approaches can be less productive.

Yet this does not mean that one must spend years practising the Eastern arts before acting or facilitating workshops. Simpler approaches are not without value, so long as their limitations are acknowledged.

One key point is that fears and concerns about futures depend on human perception and understanding. As such, the locus of power resides not in a disembodied vision but within the individuals who give it life. This, perhaps, is the unifying principle of all futures workshops; they are a means to an end, and the end is an increase in human capacity to create and affirm the visions of futures people want. When the nature of those wants, or needs, is reflected on with clarity (rather than simply assumed in a commonsensical way which merely reinforces the status quo), visioning becomes a precursor of social and cultural innovation. In other words, the necessary idealism of the imaging process can be informed and tempered by a critical review of the cultural context. Part of the essential groundwork is the analysis and renegotiation of meanings which exist as assumptions within a dominant worldview.

Renegotiation of worldview meanings and assumptions

Critical futures study suggests that some of the most productive options involve diagnosis and reconstruction at the heart of the worldview. That implies close, critical attention to presuppositions, core values and constitutive meanings. These may well be hidden, but they are no less powerful for that. They are not immutable since, to some extent, they are refashioned by, and for, each generation.

What areas could be ripe for renegotiation? One is the notion that nations are necessarily driven by technical and economic changes. A perspective which looks at *human* development seems to suggest rather different lines of innovation and change. That is why the notion of a 'wisdom culture' (see below) is useful. It provides a framework of understandings and values which begin not from an economic theory, nor from a set of technical capacities, but from a view of what it means to be human, based on the most advanced models available.

Paradoxically, such models are not exclusively modern. Huxley summarized a lot of the evidence in *The Perennial Philosophy* (1945). Since then, Maslow and the work of transpersonal psychologists have shown many paths towards higher stages of integration and development.[22] And the point of all this? Well, if we consider how much of our political, social, economic and cultural life is driven by negatives (fear, greed, violence etc) the primary role of human motives and responses becomes clear. If it were possible to reconceptualize politics, society, the economy and culture according to the highest and most advanced human motives (such as vision, clarity and what Schumacher called 'enoughness') then the entire pattern would be transformed. Could this lead to a different historical dynamic?

There are other worldview assumptions to do with temporality, growth, nature, resources, power and so on. The work of 'probing beneath the surface' in these ways, while seen as subversive by some actually seems to give access to some of the richest options for cultural adaptation. It then becomes possible to look for a different historical dynamic, one that contrasts with . . . faster . . . bigger . . . further away . . . more.[23]

'Imag-ining' a different historical dynamic

It seems clear that present-day negative views of futures are driven by fairly primitive human instincts which are magnified and augmented by powerful technologies (particularly tools of communication and the mass media). The interaction of an industrial worldview with the political and commercial opportunism of the 20th century has permitted a crass, short-sighted marketing culture to become dominant. So it is hardly surprising that a positive view of the future is lost. It cannot be overemphasized that the simple extension of present trends leads inexorably on to a devastated and impoverished world. That fact underlies all the reasons why young people get depressed and makes it clear why business-as-usual assumptions are no longer viable. We are caught up in a giddy pattern of dynamic change and chronic unsolved world problems.

Yet if Polak was right, it is entirely possible to 'breach the bounds' of present social reality and to 'imag-ine' a very different world structured according to different values and assumptions. This could be the role of a 'wisdom culture'. It may not be achieved tomorrow, next year of even next century. What it does do is much more immediate and practical. It creates a contrast which, like the best speculative fiction, de-familiarizes the present, makes it seem strange (ie historically contingent). A compelling vision therefore appears which transcends the catastrophic futures endemic to technocratic scenarios.

How can one define a wise culture? We cannot be entirely sure. Table 2 provides some possibilities, gleaned from the work of Ken Wilber.[24] The actual details are less important than *the quality of consciousness* which they evoke, for it is this which is arguably the pivot, rather than the technical or other means by which it is expressed. Nor need this quality be wholly displaced into future time. The startling thing is that people have always been capable of it. Today one such person may be Thomas Berry. His *The Dream of the Earth* seems to presage exactly the kind of shifts outlined here. Following Berman (whose book, *The Reenchantment of the World* is a milestone in this literature), he writes,

> This reenchantment with the earth as a living reality is the condition for our rescue of the earth from the impending destruction that we are imposing upon it. To carry this out

> effectively, we must now, in a sense, reinvent the human species with the community of life species. Our sense of reality and of value must consciously shift from an anthropocentric to a biocentric norm of reference . . . Our challenge is to create a new language, even a new sense of what it is to be human. It is to transcend not only national limitations, but even our species isolation, to enter the larger community of living species. This brings about a completely new sense of reality and value.[25]

Table 2. Aspects of a Wisdom Culture

- Vivid understanding of common humanity
- Move beyond roles based on race, gender etc
- Balanced use of rationality and intuition
- Higher motivations reshape economic life
- Methods and institutions to foster growth of consciousness
- Education as a discipline in transcendence
- Technology as aid to transcendence, not substitute
- Local differences set in context of universals
- All people and religions seen as one in spirit
- Governance depends upon mastery of the system at each level; body/mind/soul/spirit

Source: After Wilber, *op cit*, reference 22.

This 'new sense of reality and value' is, perhaps, the key to a new historical dynamic. In part it turns not on the intellectualization of experience, still less on the reductionist interrogation of nature by naturalistic science; but rather on *the direct experience of intrinsic value*. This stands in stark contrast to use-value and exchange-value which still remain core assumptions of the late industrial era. Imaging workshops which can bring participants to this point in living experience are clearly promoting social change at a profound level.

Intrinsic value gives back to the earth, its wildlife and ecology the right to independent existence, regardless of the needs or uses of humankind. But, as McKibben and others have pointed out, from a human viewpoint nature can be said to exist no longer as an independent category.[26] This may be overstated. Yet in order for nature to recover and retain its capacity to sustain any life it will need, in some sense, to be reconstituted at the heart of the social order. This is a difficult task . . . but not a hopeless one. It is becoming increasingly clear to many observers that the 'ecological imperative' is indeed primary. For example, Lester Milbrath writes:

> Life in a viable ecosystem is the core value of a sustainable society; that means all life, not just human life. Ecosystems function splendidly without humans but human society would die without a viable ecosystem. (Hence) we must give top priority to our ecosystem, second priority to our society; only when the viability of those two systems is assured is it permissible to seek quality of life in any way we choose.[27]

An imperative of this kind will not be easily sustained due to inertia and strong opposition from industrial-era systems and assumptions. So ways are being sought to widen the debate and transform it into a broad social process. One project which aims to do just that is Imagine the Future (ITF).

ITF is a coalition of organizations and groups in Victoria, Australia, which is based on the premise that 'if we can imagine a better world, then we can each do something to help create it'. In the words of the organizers, ITF is about:

- sharing ideas;
- taking initiatives;
- complementing programmes already begun;
- validating and celebrating people's steps toward ecological sustainability;
- resolving fears about the future; and
- establishing an appropriate structure through which these things can happen more easily.[28]

ITF is intended to be a process as well as a structure. It will involve all sections of the community, and particularly the young. It is now under the auspices of the Australian Conservation Foundation (ACF), one of the major environmental organizations in the country. The plan is to build up a constituency of support over about two years and to hold an ITF week in 1992. A small staff is working with numerous volunteers to bring about a broad spectrum of events, including conferences, lectures, exhibitions, satellite hook-ups, youth exchanges and a futures expo. If ITF week is a success it could go on to become an annual event.

ITF could be dismissed as misplaced idealism. Yet that would be a mistake. It is designed to encourage exactly the kind of broad social involvement which permits non-specialists to have their say and to contribute to a range of future-shaping actions. It will provide numerous fora for dialogue and debate. It will constitute a seedbed for social innovations. One of the latter is a series of seminars in which presenters will be encouraged to embody their suggestions in the form of desirable images. Another is a community arts project in which artists will be commissioned to create their own images of futures. This 'image bank' will itself become a catalytic resource, making otherwise abstract ideas more concrete and accessible. Such an enterprise may do more to communicate some of the core ideas of futures work than many academic papers! If successful it could become a model to be emulated elsewhere.

Conclusion

The capacity to imagine other, and different, futures is one of the defining characteristics of humankind. When properly harnessed towards shared ends it provides many of the keys to our predicament. Redundant assumptions can be discarded, values can be renegotiated, oppressive and destructive systems can be dismantled. In their place the open future is waiting to emerge. Once we give up the impossible task of trying to 'predict the future' and instead begin to participate in creating it, the foundations of informed optimism and empowerment become much clearer.

So while it remains true that violent, cynical and otherwise negative images dominate existing views of futures, it is also true that all the resources, the tools, concepts, methods etc of the futures field, along with an impressive array of non-industrial cultural resources are the inspiration and energy of people of good will, provide the wherewithal to change this otherwise depressing picture. The exhaustion of a particular worldview and its inherent possibilities in no way signals the end of human aspiration or ability. Rather, it directs us back to some of the most fundamental questions about the constitution of the social order: questions about people, nature, purpose, meaning and responsibility. Close attention to the shifting foundations of fact reveals a fascinating picture which can be taken as the outlines of a new (or renewed) cultural synthesis. Here are the most durable grounds for recovery and hope.

The basis for qualified optimism is not an illusion. It lies in the steady emergence of a 'deep consensus' about necessary changes and adaptations, in the creative potential of futures imagining processes and in the richness of cultural resources which have so far hardly been called into play. The upshot is that despite all the major challenges and crises facing us, the 21st century really could be worth living in. The transition to a sustainable society and a global culture will not be easy, but it no longer seems like a distant dream. There is no better time to consider the words of Condor speaking of his gift to humanity from the Council for All Beings:

> I, Condor, give you my keen, far-seeing eye. I see at a great distance what is there and what is coming. Use that power to look ahead beyond your day's busy-ness, to heed what you see, and plan.

(And mountain:)

> Humans, I offer you my deep peace. Come to me at any time to rest, to dream. Without dreams you may lose your vision and your hope. Come, too, for my strength and steadfastness, whenever you need them.[29]

Follow-up work

The questions arising from Chapter 4 focus on the source and nature of recent and contemporary images of the future. Such images, both positive and negative, will play a crucial role in framing our experiences of the 21st century.

1. How true do you think it is that 'contemporary views of futures tend to be not so much about the things we want to achieve as about the things we want to avoid'?
2. Explain why images of the future are so important to a society? What role do you think education should play in exploring images of preferred futures?
3. Carry out your own survey of different forms of media to establish what images of the future they implicitly or explicitly offer. You could focus either on adult images or those particularly aimed at young people. What values do they promote?
4. What visions of the future are offered by critical social movements such as those focusing on the environment, race, gender, human rights or poverty? How are these different from the visions conveyed by the popular media?
5. Write your own mini-scenario for a better future in the year 2020. How old will you be then? How do you hope things will be different? How do you hope education will be different?

Chapter 5

IMAGE AND ACTION IN PEACE BUILDING

Elise Boulding

The peace-maker's dilemma

Usually the historical record is invoked to show the inevitability of war. Indeed history (mostly written by men) is largely a story of wars won or lost. Yet the capacity to envision a human condition of peacefulness is a continuing feature of every civilization, handed down from generation to generation. The current lack of general awareness of this imagery compounds the feeling that war is inevitable. Earlier civilizations knew their 'peace stories.' The Greeks celebrated the Elysian fields where former warriors laid weapons aside and walked arm in arm through green meadows discoursing on philosophy and declaiming poetry[1]. The Norse warriors feasted and shared like brothers on the mythological plains of Ida[2]. Chinese writings described a small and sparsely populated kingdom 'where people love their lives and no one wants to move afar. . . . Fine weapons are in their possession, but no one uses them'[3]. In the ancient Hebrew prophecy, swords shall be beaten into plowshares and nation shall not lift up a sword against nation. The Christian book of Revelations speaks of the river of the water of life, where the tree of life grows, with its leaves for the healing of the nations. In the Islamic scriptures God guards humans from the evil of the day, gives them radiancy and gladness, and rewards patience with the gift of a peaceable garden[4].

These are mythic images of a condition that is a gift of the gods, but some human leaders have tried to emulate them. In the third century B.C., the Indian Emperor Ashoka dug wells and planted trees along his highways so that his subjects might walk in peace [5]. 'Peace queens' and 'peace kings' have erupted periodically in the pages of history[6], and every culture produces its own version of the imagery of peace.

Yet in the 1980s, instead of imagery of the peaceable garden, we find the bleak scenario of nuclear war and Armageddon. [A distinction needs to be made between the basic human capacity for envisioning the good and the fundamentalist perversion of that capacity in the doctrine of Armageddon, with its ensuing peaceable kingdom for the elect only. Nuclear fundamentalism as analyzed by Lifton[7] deals with that kind of perversion.]

Social psychologists concerned about the scenario of Armageddon do not look at mythic imagery of peace; rather, they map the drama of nuclear threat. Psychologists have done a good job of such mapping in the 25-year period bounded by the appearance of Kelman's *International Behavior*[8] and Lifton's *Death in Life: Survivors of Hiroshima*[9], and on the other end, by White's *Psychology of the Prevention of Nuclear War*[10]. Systems analysis, clarifying the nature of both perceptual and institutional systems relating to threat, and process analysis, dealing with the range of conflictual and integrative responses to threat, provide us with a respectable body of policy-relevant knowledge. Such maps of potential action domains, however, tend to emphasize the dilemmas of strategy and tactics in the nuclear present, and they leave largely untouched basic questions of how to move from a war-prone to a peace-prone international system. Even Lifton's work – running like a bright thread through this 25-year period with his analysis of the nuclear illusion and nuclear numbing, his exposé of nuclear fundamentalism and nuclear normalcy, and his repeated calls to action for a nuclear-free future[11, 12] – leaves the nuclear protestor struggling in the nuclear present.

Because of my own extensive peace research, I was keenly aware by the mid–1970s of the absence of clear conceptions of what kind of world would be possible and sustainable under conditions of substantial disarmament. Researchers and activists alike were concerned with controlling the arms race and reducing the role of the military in international disputes, but what kind of world were they working toward? It gradually dawned on me that people could not really imagine a world without military defence systems. Not being able to picture an alternative, they turned to short-term survival strategies rather than focusing on processes of long-range social change.

The purpose of this chapter is to describe and analyze one specific technique for creating mental images of a peaceful world and related action scenarios, known as 'Imaging a World Without Weapons Workshops.' Before turning to the workshops, however, I discuss Polak's theory of the image of the future as an agent of social change, and relate it to the concept of image as used in psychology.[13]

The historical function of images of the future

Fred Polak was one of the first thinkers to call attention to the atrophy of our capacity to visualize a wholly different future. His *Image of the Future* was written for a Europe paralyzed by the experience of World War II. Our nuclear paralysis in the 1980s seems a continuation of that condition. As Polak's translator, I increasingly came to feel his theory of the role of societal imaging in the historical process, and his diagnosis of a decline in the West's imaging capacity[14], were relevant to the inability of policy makers, scholars, activists, and the general public to picture a humanly desirable postnuclear world.

According to Polak, the human capacity to create mental images of the 'totally other' – that which has never been experienced or recorded – is the key dynamic of history. At every level of awareness, from the individual to the macrosocietal, imagery is continuously generated about the 'not-yet.' Such imagery inspires our intentions, which then move us purposefully forward. Through their daily choices of action, individuals, families, enterprises, communities, and nations move toward that which they imagine to be a desirable tomorrow. Polak points out, however, that historically alternating waves of optimism and pessimism about reality roll through time, as do alternating views about the end of the world. Sometimes humans are seen as partners with God or Nature, other times as helpless objects of supernatural action.

In Polak's reading of history, optimism about reality combined with a utopian sense of human empowerment set in motion a powerful dynamic. Utopian optimism has characterized the Western worldview of recent centuries – but not of the last few decades. In eras when pessimism combines with a sense of cosmic helplessness, the quality of human intentionality declines and, with it, the quality of imagery of the not-yet. Societies in that condition live bounded by the present, with no social dynamic for change available to them. This is our situation in the post-World War II Western world.

The image concept in social science

When psychologists talk about images in relation to international conflict, it is frequently in terms of mental representations of nation states, particularly stereotypic representations. Perception of the adversary is a key concept. The use of *image* in relation to the future does not involve a radical break with that tradition, but rather its extension into another dimension. Kelman's definition of *image* as 'the organized representation of an object in an individual's cognitive system' encompasses K. Boulding's broad use of the term in his book *The Image*,[15] which was in turn based on Polak's work. Thus the term *image* includes conceptions of the represented object in the past and future as well as the present; in short, images have associated memories and expectations. They may vary in the number of constituent elements, be more or less rich, complex, or differentiated. In their fantasy aspect, they go well beyond actual experiences of the imager[16]. They may, as Jervis[17] and White[18] have shown in their analyses of misperception, be organized in ways that produce pathologically hostile interactions between holders of competing sets of images.

Deutsch's[19] use of the image concept in his study of changing images of international conflict provides another link to the usage in this article. He wrote of a 'virtual coalition of war-promoting images', including images of war as a Darwinian necessity, as God ordained, as a rationalist strategy, all summed up in an Armageddon concept that sounds strikingly familiar in 1986. He asked, in 1966, where the possible coalitions were among holders of potentially peace-promoting images, and he found no clear answer.

The work of Fiske, Pratto, and Pavelchak[20] posed a related question: To what extent does imagery about nuclear war trigger antinuclear activism? In an ingenious study involving a telephone survey eliciting images of nuclear war, they tested the traditional predictors of activism – general political activism, attitudes toward the issue in question, the salience of the issue, and beliefs about the probability of the issue-related event (i.e., nuclear war). Fiske et al. added to these traditional predictors the categories of concreteness of imagery, availability (readiness of articulation) of imagery, and another measure of salience, and they found that all except readiness of articulation correlate with self-reported levels of antinuclear activism. Their results indicated that under certain conditions, when the negative images developed are especially concrete, individuals can apparently be motivated to antinuclear activity.

In the framework presented here, the question is raised about the effect on people's actions of positive imagery of a possible desired world rather than negative images of a feared world. If negative imagery about a feared future can produce positive action, what will positive imagery about a desired future produce?

Generating peace imagery

The idea of generating imagery about a peaceful world and examining its action potentials can be related to level-of-aspiration studies, which identify personal images of the future and examine their effects on personal behaviour. McClelland, Atkinson, Clark, & Lowell[21] and Atkinson[22] have shown that levels of aspiration about personal performance (i.e., images of how the individual expects to perform at a future moment) are predictive of actual performance, both in Western countries and in countries undergoing modernization. It seems being able to picture a desired future is empowering in the present. The hypothesis that picturing a functioning disarmed world can empower creative action seems to deserve exploration in the light of these earlier findings.

The representational work associated with what is here called *imaging* can range from free-floating fantasy and escapist day-dreaming to the conscious reworking of sleeping dreams – i.e., 'lucid dreaming'[23] – and visualization as a healing therapy in illness. Focused, self-directed imaging of a desired societal future is the special form of intentional imaging considered here. A critical feature of both personal and social therapeutic imaging is that the imager must be able to picture significant details of a well person or of a healthy society. The language of therapy, however, is too limiting for the much broader functions of social imaging. Here, the significant aspect of imaging is that human beings construct social reality in their minds prior to the sociophysical task of constructing the external reality.

Imaging and the imagination

The human imagination can be thought of as a problem-solving faculty, continually reworking experience by means of image formation. The more critical the problem, the more salient the reworking process. A lifetime of sensory experience provides part, but only part, of the raw materials for the imaging process.

People have to be encouraged to image, taught to exercise a capacity they are unaccustomed to using in a disciplined way. The obstacles to imaging lie partly in our social institutions, including the schools – which discourage imaging because it can lead to imagined alternatives that challenge existing social arrangements – and partly in the minds of a generation unskilled in using capacities long ignored.

The basic hypothesis of this chapter and of the workshops to be described is that those capacities can be reengaged. The widespread interest in meditation techniques offers a starting point. Imaging, like meditation, requires an emptying of the mind. At the same time it 'works in the middle of all senses and puts experience together in a living and breathing object-structure'[24].

In turning to the imaging workshops as image- and action-generating techniques, we will explore the following questions: (1) *Can* people, in fact, image a hopeful future in an appropriately facilitative environment? (2) What are some of the kinds of imagery produced in such situations? Corollary questions are: (3) What is the relevance of previous life experience and orientation to the types of imagery that arise? (4) Will shared orientations add to the concreteness of the imagery? (5) Is there any evidence that feelings of action readiness are generated by those images?

An experiment in imaging: picturing a world without weapons

During 1981–1982 Warren Ziegler and I held a series of experimental workshops combining Polak's theories and a practical problem-solving technique involving futures invention developed by Ziegler[25, 26]. Peace movement networks were originally used for recruiting participants, but the circle soon widened to include people who were concerned with issues of nuclear war but who did not necessarily identify themselves as peace activists. Participants included scientists, teachers, ministers, artists, community workers, and students, ranging in age from the late teens to the eighties. They were asked to discover a viable social order that functions without (conventionally defined) weapons.

Since that experimental year, training workshops have been held, and an association of workshop facilitators has been formed to carry on workshops. Imaging is a highly individual process, so facilitators develop differing styles, but the overall pattern has remained basically the same. In involves using a workbook with a sequence of exercises providing a balanced alternation of individual imaging, analytic work in small groups, and plenary discussions of what is happening.

Workshop procedures

The methodology of the workshop is based on Polak's concept of a 'breach in time,' a drastic discontinuity between present and future that can nevertheless be encompassed by the human imagination. Participants must step, in fantasy, into a future very different from the present, and report back from that future on their observations of a society, which they must then analyze in terms of the social institutions that could sustain it. Subsequently, they must account for that future by an imagined history of the society. This is very demanding work, drawing alternately on fantasy and on analysis, and requiring suspension of pessimism and disbelief. The workshop takes participants through a series of steps, from an initial 'wish list' for the future to a final action plan in the present. These steps are outlined in a workbook handed to each participant, which includes space to write and to draw ideas and images that occur at each stage. During the workshop, however, the emphasis is on oral instruction rather than reading the written explanations.

The wish list. Since participants generally find it more difficult to give themselves permission to observe what they *hope* will happen, rather than what they fear, the first task given them is to draw up a wish list for the future. What would they like to see in the best possible future they can imagine? This task directly addresses a major obstacle to the imaging process: People want to be 'realistic,' and they take it as axiomatic that fears are realistic and hopes unrealistic. The individual's wish list serves to guide the imaging process once the future has been entered.

Recalling a childhood memory. A second obstacle to imaging is uncertainty as to what the process is like. People are asked to 'step into' a happy childhood memory, reexperiencing it in the imagination. These memories are then related aloud, and the suggestion made that, however the past memory was presented to the mind, the same process will be at work in creating mental representations of the not-yet-experienced.

Stepping into the future. Now it is time to step into the future; the time leap required is 30 years. This span is chosen because it will be within the lifetime of most participants, but is far enough away that major changes can come about. Only one basic fact about this future world is given: It is, for all practical purposes, free of weapons.

Participants are reminded that drastic changes have previously happened in similar 30-year historical time frames: e.g., the dismantling of the British Empire, the shift from a 50-nation to a 150-nation world, the advent of a worldwide electronic communication network. A suspension of disbelief is required of the participant. No matter how the abolition of weapons has occurred, *it has happened,* and participants are now to report what they see in that world.

After being instructed to relax and close their eyes, participants mentally follow the workshop facilitator out the front door of the building they are in and are then confronted with a high hedge stretching as far as they can see in either direction. They are instructed to get to the other side of the hedge any way they can – that is where the future lies. Various suggestions are made about how to move around in that 'future present moment,' how they can find settlements, informants, etc. Every effort is made to help them enter the experience of *being there*. The words *imaging, imagining, fantasizing, daydreaming, reverie* are all used since different words work for different people in assisting them into the fantasy mode. At the same time they are fantasizing, they are also encouraged to remember the wish list at the back of their minds. This is to help them see what they hope for rather than what they fear. They may talk to people they meet in the future or may be silent observers, as they wish. Some who have trouble 'seeing' anything are encouraged to look for people or places they knew 30 years ago. Participants are urged to look very carefully to see what makes this world 'tick' – to see how people live, work, play, handle conflict, etc., and to make notes in their workbooks about what they see.

Sharing images. When people have returned from their visit to the future, they describe what they have seen in groups of two or three, to help solidify their experience.

World construction, phase 1. Continuing in groups of two or three, individuals are instructed to consider the fantasy fragments they have 'seen' as indicators of a social structure that they must now analytically reconstruct. An important part of this process is to make pictorial, diagrammatic, or schematized narrative representations of the future world that one has experienced. The suggestion is made to focus the representation on the key themes or most salient features of that world. All individuals make their own depictions on large sheets of paper.

World construction, phase 2. Groups of five are formed, based on perceived theme similarity in individual world constructions. They are instructed to develop a common scenario of their experienced future world, which is also to be depicted visually on paper. Merging different perceptions in a common scenario is challenging and involves much dialogue, negotiation, and compromise. The dialogue also helps test the validity of the images, since each is subjected to critical questioning by colleagues. In developing their common depiction on paper, few teams rely on words alone to convey their imaged future. Graphic talent varies widely, of course. All groups are encouraged to note somewhere on the sheet the key concepts involved in their depictions. In this way symbolic meanings can be more fully captured by outside observers.

Remembering history. After the groups have enjoyed inspecting and discussing each other's futures in a plenary session, participants are requested to become historians. They now individually record historical happenings. Standing in the 'future present moment' of their fantasy experience, they must now work their way back, in imagination, to the actual present. What happened 'last year?' Five years ago? and so on back through three decades. Subsequently, they do the same in their groups. The blend of eidetic imagery and intellectual inquiry, which has characterized the work of constructing the future, also continues in the tracing of social process back to the present. Creating group histories out of disparate and often contradictory individual rememberings involves another round of dialogue, negotiation, and compromise.

Action planning for the present. Given the futures they have pictured and the history they have remembered, participants now consider what action they might take in the present to bring about the desired future. This planning is done in the context of analyzing the 'action spaces' available to each in the present, given who they are, what they do in their daily lives, and with whom they interact. Participants are encouraged to come up with a specific action plan for one of their action spaces – in a home, neighbourhood, workplace, school, or community setting.

Three case examples

Three different workshop groups have been chosen as exemplars, to help answer the general questions about whether people can image hopeful futures, and if so, what futures they image. These exemplars will also help answer the additional questions that came out of the early workhops: When people are brought together on the basis of more specifically focused interests, rather than a general interest in peace, will the imaging themes be different?

Will the futures have more concrete and action-generating details? What kinds of action ideas will be produced?*

Group profiles
The three groups described all experienced one three-hour-long workshop, each conducted in 1985. They were all groups that had some additional purpose for being together besides the workshop itself, so little time had to be spent on helping the group to function cooperatively. The first was a conference group sponsored by the American Friends Service Committee in New York City on the changing role of men, the second an international youth conference on peace, and the third a continuing group of scholars working on models of a warless world. In each case, participants were encouraged to draw consciously on their own experience and knowledge in entering the fantasy mode to picture a world without weapons.

Conference on changing roles of men. Participants came to this conference to examine how existing gender roles affect society, and to develop a vision of a changed society freed from gender-based oppression. The over 100 participants who joined the workshop, roughly equal numbers of men and women, had a specific interest in the link between gender-role change and peace. All New Yorkers in a variety of professional and clerical occupations, they ranged in age from the early 20s to the 50s. The men's movement, feminist, and gay-lesbian organizations were represented.

Pax Humana group. Linking the 1985 UN Year of Youth and the 1986 UN Year of Peace, the theme of this conference, held on the University of Ottawa campus, was 'a commitment to creating peace.' Four hundred young people between 18 and 30 – from 50 or more countries from all continents – had been brought together

* In the early experimental workshops we conducted, with people of diverse interests and only a concern for peace in common, the picture that emerged tended to be of a localist world with a strong sense of planetary consciousness, a world in which food and agriculture were important, and various high-tech/low-tech combinations of rural-urban living in a context of strong transnational networking had been developed. Nation states were less important, and new international structures were emerging that fit with local autonomy. Few operational details of how such a society might function emerged. The images were broad and sweeping. The action ideas that emerged were similarly rather general.

through UN associations, scouting and other youth organizations, and exchange programmes. The conference was conducted in French, Spanish, and English, with interpreters available for other languages.

About 200 of the participants came to the university gymnasium where the workshop was held. Needless to say, the diversity of cultural backgrounds was enormous. Large-, small-, and medium-sized countries were represented. Some young men and women came from rural tribes, others from capital cities. Some came from countries torn by civil war, others from highly stable societies. Some came from ancient civilizations, others from 'new' countries. Some were colonizers, some colonized; some from one of the superpower alliance blocs, others from nonaligned countries. All were highly motivated by the unusual nature of their gathering.

EXPRO. The Exploratory Project on the Conditions of Peace, formed in 1984, is a group of about two dozen academics, intellectuals, and activists committed to making war obsolete, to identifying the elements of a peace system, and to finding the means for creating it. The majority of the members are political scientists, historians, or sociologists, and they find conceptual analysis and model building more congenial than mental activity in a fantasy mode. Ranging in age from 40 to 70, this group of one-third women and two-thirds men has tried to reach beyond its own middle-class, white, liberal background. Twelve participated in the workshop, but as some imagery material was lost, information on themes are only available for eight persons. This is a very small group compared to the first two, but its distinctive scholarly character makes it interesting for comparative purposes.

Method of analysis

Because formal research hypotheses were not established in advance of the workshops, this report describes a highly exploratory investigation. The analysis was based on inspection of the sheets prepared by three- to five-person working groups in each workshop, attempting to convey their common futures. The groups had been instructed to include words in their depictions to name the key themes of their future, and these key words became important guides for me in interpreting the pictures. My system of analysis involved listing each separate concept, theme, or characteristic that appeared on the group sheets, and then counting their frequency of appearance. Each representation contained several themes, so there were many more themes than sheets. Theme categories were then combined to make a more manageable list. In addition to listing types of concepts and characteristics, I analyzed the *mode* of representation.

An important additional source of information about the images of the future generated by the participants came from listening in on team discussions of visualizations and also from plenary discussions of particularly strong images. Because of the three-hour time constraint on these workshops (full-length workshops take a day and a half or longer), participants did not have time to develop their future history and present action programme on paper. Instead, this was handled through plenary discussion, and my account of this part of the workshop is based only on my own notes.

What happened in the workshops?

The answer to our first question – *can* people image a hopeful future in an appropriately facilitative environment – is *yes*. We will examine the types of imagery generated in the workshops.

Image themes

Here are the initial impressions of these visitors to the future when they first come through the hedge: Some find a village or a farm, some find a city, but there are certain features of this world that they all identify at once. Whatever people are doing, women and men are doing it together. Children and the elderly seem to be everywhere – there is no age segregation. Communities are also described as racially mixed. Learning seems to take place 'on the job.'

This is a nonhierarchical world; no one is 'in charge'. It is also one in which locality is very important. Connections with other localities are gradually discovered, but the first impression is of a strong sense of place. Community gardens and local growing of food are widely seen, with larger farms in the hinterlands. Technology is low profile, but it does exist and everyone reports that it is shared. There are no technological haves and have-nots. Interestingly, production technologies are rarely mentioned. The technologies described usually involve communication and transport. Computers turn out to be omnipresent, and are a major knowledge resource in the localist society. They are also the source of social connectedness, as discovered in later imagery about a world council linking local communities. If nation-states are present, they do not play a role in the visualization until the analytic stage is reached. Although the new-consciousness theme varies in importance, there is widespread reporting that people are operating out of a different sense of awareness than that of 1985. Some report strong currents of 'cosmic awareness'; others feel it primarily in terms of an increase in interpersonal security and a general inclination to peaceableness.

What has been described so far are features common not only to all three of the groups included in this analysis, but common to most imaging groups I have worked with. These features may be thought of as the baseline future. Moving on to features that are not universal, we find the following themes, listed in their order of importance to the imagers.

Two striking image sets stand out. One is of 'a boundaryless world' (the term *boundaryless* recurred several times both in discussion and on paper). Boundarylessness is conceived as an awareness of a free flow of people and thoughts and activities, unimpeded by formal structures or by occupational and political barriers. People in the men's group thought of this as 'rolelessness,' absence of social pressure, with little distinction between work and play. The youth group tended to think of it in terms of a free flow of cultures around the world, with no national demarcations.

The second striking image set concerns a 'bright, clean, green' world with clear blue oceans. The adjectives *bright, clean, green* recurred repeatedly for both the men's group and the young people. The images convey a sense of beauty and reverence, and feelings of closeness to the earth that have an almost tactile quality. This was most pronounced among the young people.

Another vivid set of images pertains to the 'feel' of the local community. The presence of others is felt as a joyful, nurturing experience. This is a world in which everyone belongs, in which people delight in caring for others. This comes through in descriptions of celebrations witnessed, with singing and dancing, in descriptions of how people mingle during everyday activities, and in descriptions of the expressions on their faces.

A less prominent theme, but not infrequently reported, is of community services formally structured so that every kind of personal need is taken care of – food, health care, employment, personal growth. This degree of structure contradicts the earlier-mentioned imagery of boundarylessness and free-flowing interpersonal nurturance, but it also reflects many 1980s' wish lists for better social services in the future.

One other theme has great importance for some participants (mainly in the men's roles group) – the theme of family. When these participants enter 2015, they immediately see people in family groups; the whole community is apparently organized into large extended family households.

The remaining themes were reported by only a few participants. Language is one minor theme. Some imagers discover everyone in the world speaking the same language, others find that the individuals they meet are multilingual. Work and education are two other themes. Those who observe the occupations of inhabitants of the future find that working hours no longer exist as they did in 1985. Work itself is voluntary, with flexible hours, and has the characteristics of craft activity. Those who observe educational activities can find no school buildings. Learning appears integrated into other community activities. Observers conclude that in this world everyone is a learner, and that education is lifelong.

Some observers find an upside-down quality to this world. The old North-South polarities no longer exist. The countries of the South are flourishing. Hunger, poverty and sickness have disappeared. In contrast, the North has slowed down.

Image differences among workshop groups

Image themes varied substantially between groups, as Table 1 with its rank ordering of themes for each of the three groups makes dramatically clear. The men's roles group, with primarily interpersonal concerns, focused on extended family households as living/learning/work/play spaces providing the setting for a free-flowing boundaryless urban lifestyle. The metropolis was transformed into a garden city on a human scale maintained by soft technology.

In the analytic phase of the workshop, the men's roles group devised institutional structures to support small-scale home-based production and production-linked learning. Community centres took care of coordination, conflict resolution, and housing the computer facilities that brought needed information to the city. These folks were homebodies. Travel was unimportant, and the existence of an international entity was shadowy.

Among the Pax Humana young people, many had journeyed from far places and had dealt with government bureaucracies to attend the gathering in Ottawa.

Table 1. Key Images of a Desirable Future World Expressed in Three Different Workshops (Frequency of Appearance Expressed as Ranks)

Image	Workshop-Group		
	Pax Humana (51 Newsprints)	Men's roles (48 Newsprints)	EXPRO (8 Newsprints)
Boundarylessness: Free flows of all kinds	1	4[a,b]	–
Equality, nonhierarchy, human rights	2	4[a,b]	4
Location, agriculture, food sharing	3	1	2.5[b]
Clean, green, bright environment	4.5[b]	8	–
World council	4.5[b]	11	2.5[b]
Peaceful, celebratory, nurturant society	6	4[b]	–
New consciousness, unity of creation	7	10	5
High Tech: Sharing lifestyle	8	6	6
Human services for all	9.5[b]	7	–
Multilinguality, or one world language	9.5[b]	–	–
Familistic world	11	2	–
Work: Creative, voluntary, flexitime	–	9	–
Experiential education, life-long learning	–	4[b]	–
Shift in North-South relations	–	–	1

[a]For the men's roles group, the boundarylessness and equality categories are combined, since the participants used boundarylessness primarily to refer to equal or shared interpersonal relations.

[b]Image categories that appeared with the same frequency are given the same rank.

The adventure of travel permeated the future world they saw. Like the men's roles world, it had no national boundaries, but this was a different kind of boundarylessness. People of all colours and languages were on the road, journeying, speaking many languages and understanding one another. Houses had open doors. Everywhere they went, food was being grown, harvested, shared, and there was a constant traffic of people and food between country and town. The absence of hunger was a major theme.

There was green and blue everywhere in these young people's images – green forests, green farmlands, green town gardens, and blue lakes and oceans. For all the happy bustle and movement and open doors, families as such were rarely observed. In the world construction phase, a regionally linked world governing council appeared. The youth group seemed to enjoy inventing local service and regulatory structures, and they thought in terms of regional institutions and of linkage systems, from the local to the regional to the world council.

The EXPRO group had a harder time with the fantasy mode than the other two groups, probably because they came to the workshop with already well-defined ideas about future world structures. They did, however, 'find' a world with familiar political landmarks changed. The countries of the South were now sharing in the leadership formerly exercised by the North. Some EXPRO participants saw a politically redesigned high-technology/post-industrial world, with an effective international conflict-control machinery and reduced national sovereignty, but it was hard for them to see its human details. They were able to devise an organizational chart showing how it functioned, but they did not experience it. Other EXPRO members were able to visit local communities and discover people happily networking around the world from their own village, and tending their 'clean green' gardens. Rather than organizational charts, the EXPRO localists drew complicated networks showing how ideas, institutions, and people interconnected.

It is certainly clear that the imagery of each group related to their past experience and major concerns. The city-dwelling men's roles group saw a transformed, humanized city; the international young people saw a shining green world with open roads and abundant food; and EXPRO members found a new world order. Each pictured a world in which the major problems they were concerned with had been solved.

The significance of shared orientations among participants

Did the participants' shared orientations enhance the quality of imagery in each group? In two cases, the previously shared interests may have been a handicap in that they reduced the range of imagery generated and limited the type of detail evoked. The men's roles group had difficulty moving from interpersonal relations to thinking structurally and globally. Conversely, the EXPRO group had trouble moving from global structure to focusing on local detail. The shared interests of the youth were of a different kind, based on the initiation of a new international youth network for peace. The cultural diversity of this group was great, and the result was a rich and varied imagery and a fascination with structural detail.

Action readiness in terms of image intensity

It appears that shared interest alone is not enough to generate pictures of the future that are sufficiently concrete to provide a guide to action. The only real test of the extent of action readiness following the workshop experience would be to do a follow-up study some time later on actions taken. However, in lieu of such longitudinal data, instead I use two indicators of action readiness: (1) image intensity or concreteness, and (2) image saliency or relevance to personal life, as revealed in the character of the action suggestions that emerged during the final action-planning stage of the workshop.

The intensity of the imaging experience is conveyed by the use of words and pictures to depict the world of 2015. The intensity of the imaging experience was different for each of the three groups. The men's roles group certainly pictured the new human-scale city in some detail, but they used few symbols and few attempts at pictures. Rather they relied on lists and charts to convey the future world. The action-planning suggestions that came at the end were largely projected continuations of activities they were already engaged in.

The EXPRO group had trouble picturing actual scenes of people doing things, and this was reflected in the depictions of 2015, which consisted largely of charts, diagrams, and networks. There was certainly interest in giving the world system shape, but these participants were already working on futures design. Their fantasies did not produce imagery that surprised them. At most they experienced the atmospherics of more effective world governance and of changed North-South relations. Like the men's roles group, EXPRO participants were reinforced in continuing their present activities when it was time for action planning. No new directions appeared.

The young-adult group was the most affected by the imaging process. The vividness of their experience of the future was reflected both in the concrete language they used in their working teams and in what they put on paper to depict their world. Because their imagery was so vivid, I will describe it in some detail. The symbol of the world circle was the major vehicle to express their experience, and it appeared in the majority of the papers. Some were drawn as twin circles: the bad old weapons-bristling, dump-reeking, people-hurting world, side by side with the good new world of smiling people planting gardens and playing. Other depictions were of village life, with happy people dancing and working. Many papers actually showed joined hands around the world, ingeniously indicating cultural and geographic diversity behind the joined hands. There were other kinds of circular linkages: linked houses, villages, continents – in one case heads of state were linked. Readily identifiable symbols of different ideologies and religions were also depicted as linked in the world circle. One very sophisticated drawing conveyed the sense of an underlying world rhythm, shown by a vibrating triangle 'echoing' into the cultural, social, and political institutions of the future. (Two depictions were of a sad, fearful, inactive world. A striking contrast to all the others, they conveyed quiet resignation.) Notable in the great majority of representations were 'grace notes,' which decorated the main picture – musical notes, singing birds, flowers, sunbeams, hearts. Almost every picture contained trees and other growing things, and water.

It should be kept in mind that because of the three-hour time constraint on the workshop, the individual world construction phase was highly abbreviated, and the groups went straight to doing depictions. Whether the same types of representations would have appeared if every participant had first done a separate picture, it is not possible to say.

The theme of linkage so persistently depicted had at least four dimensions: (1) governance; (2) the interrelatedness of cultural, political, economic, religious, and social institutions; (3) person-to-person interrelatedness, and (4) the interrelatedness of human beings and nature.

The vividness and concreteness of the young-adults' imagery, and its strong cognitive content as well, suggests strong action readiness. This was confirmed by the highly specific action agendas for the coming year developed during the action-planning phase. These included developing national and regional youth networks to introduce peace-action ideas to the organizations each participant represented in their part of the world, and forming a youth peace and environmental council to continue the Pax Humana work.

Action readiness in terms of image saliency

Another related action-predisposing factor according to Fiske et al. is image saliency, or relevance to one's personal life situation. While all three groups had a strong concern for peace, their members were in different life stages. Most of the men's roles group and all EXPRO members were launched on their careers, and not at any particular choice point in their lives. For the Pax Humana youth, however, the workshop experience came at a critical moment in their lives. Important choices lay ahead about personal careers and directions. This greatly heightened the salience of the imaged future for them. The survival of an international youth network beyond the conference itself depended on the action decisions of the group. It is, in fact, the general experience of imaging workshop leaders that when they are working with a group that is in process of developing or changing its identity, a much higher level of action readiness is generated than when the workshop is just one more group experience.

The sense of being drawn toward action is not, however, the only possible effect of a workshop. There is another kind of long-run salience – the feeling that there is a future to work for and a generalized affirmation of commitment to that future. This is a less dramatic type of empowerment, but one that nearly all imaging workshop participants report in postworkshop debriefing sessions – in three groups studied here and in workshop groups generally.

The time factor in generating salience should also be mentioned. The temporal constraints of a three-hour workshop meant that none of our groups had sufficient time to develop the details of the future world. Specific action planning depends on 'new information' about the future sufficiently compelling to alter strategies followed in the present. A two- or three-day workshop allows for the developments of that new kind of information. Probably both the men's roles group and EXPRO would have generated more action-compelling information about the future had they worked at it longer. Because the youth group's action readiness was already high, time limitations did not affect its responsiveness.

Conclusions and implications

It is clear that people brought together to image a peaceable future world can do so. In these three workshops people generated a variety of pictures of a world very different from the one they knew, a less stressful, 'clean and green' world. Because of the deliberate emphasis on each participant's physical presence *in the future*, initial imagery tends to be of local community scenes, small town or urban. In the course of the workshop, through discussion, the implications for the larger social order are gradually spelled out; e.g., implications for education, political and economic structures, communication patterns, and arrangements for the management of conflict or violence.

Shared background or common purposes do not by themselves facilitate the generation of action-inspiring imagery. In fact, if the groups are too homogeneous, this may reduce the variety of the imagery produced. Data from the Pax Humana group suggest that some combination of common purposes and diversity of backgrounds appears desirable for enhancing the image-action connection.

There is some evidence of a possible relation among vividness or concreteness of imagery, intensity of affect, and action readiness. While more time for imaging work might increase vividness, intensity, and specificity, it also appears that salience of the issue in terms of the life stage of the participating individual or of the group affects the quality of the imaging experience.

In the context of this chapter's theme of 'promoting positive approaches to peace,' it would seem that imaging workshops have a useful role. In the three workshops described, as in nearly all imaging workshops, people arrived feeling ineffective in the face of the nuclear threat and disbelieving about disarmament; they departed empowered to varying degrees by their own imagery. Empirical determination of the actual action readiness of participants goes beyond the scope of this study, however, and it needs to be more fully explored in the future.

We know little about imaging itself, let alone about the link between image and action. At one level the connection appears obvious, for everyday experience seems to confirm that image precedes action. In the morning we mentally rehearse our expectations for our day, and our images of what is to come organize our behaviour. But what do we mean by 'image'? It need not necessarily imply visualization. A significant number of people get along without visual imagery as part of their mental constructs. Fortunately, Kelman's concept of 'organized representation of an object' leaves room for nonvisual ways of organizing such representations. The important thing is that there is some internal act of constructing a representation of a future state. If the construction is visual, the process seems obvious, but a nonvisual construction can also be representational.

The recurrence of what might be called baseline futures in the imagery produced by most workshop participants, regardless of background or setting, suggests that there may be deep structures at work in the futures-imaging process that should be more fully explored. This may be thought of in terms of Jungian archetypes[27] or the deep structures concept as used in Chomsky's[28] analysis of the development of language[29] Polak thought of futures imaging as a basic mental capacity in humans for conceiving the 'other and better,' for utopianism. Collecting and analyzing the records of a number of imaging workshops should throw important light on this process.

What is the meaning of imaging a desirable future in an Armageddon-fixated era? Can discernment and value choices be effectively linked to fantasy, avoiding both the traps of fundamentalist conceptions of the future and of substituting fantasy for action? The 'feel-good' aspects of empowerment so widely reported by workshop participants are potentially harmful if they are not harnessed to concrete action in the real world. What needs to be done to ensure that such harnessing takes place? Put another way, imaging alone does not determine the future, since many different images coexist at any one time. So what does it mean to be an image generator? In short, what is the link between imaging and social process?

Understanding the image-action nexus appears as a pressing research issue. It is particularly important to understand that connection in relation to fear-of-nuclear-war issues. Does imaging a *desirable* future increase action readiness to a level beyond that generated by fear alone? Does it change the imager's action agenda? What is the association among vividness and concreteness of futures imagery, emotional affect, salience of the issue, and the quality of ensuing social action? We urgently need long-term follow-up studies of workshop participants to identify the outcomes of their imaging experience.

How important is imagery as a 'strategy' in the peace movement? Does the effort to introduce fantasy downplay the necessity for empirical investigation of the present and for rational analytic thinking about the future? What is the ideal balance between imaginative, intuitive exploration of future possibilities, and calculating, strategic analysis?

For World Without Weapons Workshops to become an important part of peace movement strategy, more research is needed on action outcomes and on workshop procedures. As I have indicated, time pressures increasingly force workshop leaders to hold condensed three-hour imaging sessions such as the ones described here, although experience indicates that better image materials, better analytic work, and more precise action commitments come from longer workshops. Is it wise to give in to these pressures? What are the alternatives? And if three-hour workshops are to continue, what is the best use of time, given that each step of the workshop experience has to be truncated?

Regardless of how these questions are answered, imaging workshops are becoming an increasing part of peace movement activities, due in no small measure to their psychologically empowering effect. If imaging a world at peace really helps in the peace-building process, it is time for the research community to begin studying the workshop phenomenon so that an ancient tool of the imagination can be redeveloped and used in the best possible way.

Follow-up work

The questions arising from Chapter 5 all deal with the crucial importance of being able to envision the futures that we want. If we are not able to create images of more just and sustainable futures then we are not likely to be able to bring such futures about.

1. 'It seems being able to picture a desired future is empowering in the present.' Can you give examples of this from your own life experience and the experience of others?
2. Draw up your own wish list for the future. What would you like to see in the best possible future that you can imagine? What would others like to see? How similar or different is this to your own list?
3. How do the common images of preferred futures described by Elise Boulding on pages 73–75 compare with those in your own wish list? How do they compare with the lists of others?
4. Carry out a group brainstorm on each of the four dimensions of interrelatedness described on page 80. Which dimension interests you most? How can you help others to explore and appreciate the importance of such examples of interdependence?
5. Education for responsible citizenship is in part about 'action readiness.' What evidence of such readiness can you identify in a) your own peer group; b) any other group you know well? How might you be able to critically enhance such readiness for participation in democratic processes?

Chapter 6

A SUSTAINABLE FUTURE

Lester R. Brown

Throughout our lifetimes, expanding economic activity has shaped environmental trends, often altering the Earth's natural systems in ways not obvious at the time. Now, we are moving into a period where the environmental changes we have set in motion increasingly will be shaping economic trends.

Each year, the earth's forest cover grows smaller while the deserts grow larger. Each year, the amount of top-soil on our croplands diminishes, and the stratospheric ozone layer that protects us from harmful ultraviolet radiation is depleted. Each year, the concentrations of heat-trapping gases in the atmosphere rise and the number of plant and animal species shrinks. The economic effects of the environmental degradation of the planet are already affecting world food production. All forms of environmental degradation, ranging from soil erosion to the hotter summers projected as the world warms, affect agriculture adversely.

The detrimental economic consequences of environmental degradation are no longer hypothetical. They can be seen in both Africa and Latin America where a combination of rapid population growth, environmental degradation, and rising external debt have contributed to falling living standards throughout the eighties. Both Africa and Latin America ended the eighties with lower living standards and more hunger than they had when the decade began.

After a point, environmental degradation and economic decline begin to feed on each other. If we have not reversed some of these trends by the end of the nineties, the downward spiral of environmental degradation and economic decline could spread to large areas of the world. That's the bad news. The good news is that public awareness of the extent and effects of the degradation of the planet is rising everywhere. This, combined with the ending of the Cold War, provides hope for redefining security, for recognizing that the real threats to our future come more from the environmental degradation of the planet than from military aggression.

Building an environmentally sustainable global economy, one that satisfies our needs without jeopardizing the prospects of future generations, will be a massive undertaking. Unfortunately no models of sustainability exist today. For the past several decades, most developing nations have aspired to the automobile-centred, fossil-fuel-driven economies of the industrial West. But from the localized problems of intractable air pollution to the global threat of climate change, it is now clear that these societies are far from durable; indeed they are rapidly bringing about their own demise.

Successfully structuring a sustainable society requires that we have some vision of what it would look like, how it would function. If not fossil fuels to power society, then what? If forests are no longer to be cleared to grow food, then how is a larger population to be fed? If a throwaway culture leads inevitably to pollution and resource depletion, how can we satisfy our material needs? In sum, if the present path is so obviously unsound, what picture of the future can we use to guide our actions toward a global community that can endure?

Describing the shape of a sustainable society is a risky proposition. Ideas and technologies yet unknown will fill in many of the gaps. But just as any technology of flight, however primitive or advanced, must abide by the basic principles of aerodynamics, so must a lasting society satisfy some immutable criteria. With that understanding and from the experience garnered in recent decades, it is possible to describe an environmentally sustainable global economy, one that will yield a society quite different, indeed preferable to today's.

Time to get the world on a sustainable path is rapidly running out. We believe that if humanity achieves sustainability, it will do so within the next forty years. If we have not succeeded by then, environmental deterioration and economic decline will be feeding on each other, pulling us into a downward spiral of social decay and political upheaval. At such a point, reclaiming any hope of a sustainable future may simply be impossible. Our vision therefore looks to the year 2030, a time closer to the present than the end of World War II.

Sketching the outlines of a sustainable society requires some basic assumptions. First, new technologies will of course be developed. Forty years ago, for example, some renewable energy technologies now on the market did not even exist. Under the pressure of finding a means to slow global warming, researchers are likely to develop a range of new energy technologies, some of which may be difficult to imagine at the moment. In the interest of being conservative, however, the future we sketch is based only on existing technologies and foreseeable improvements in them.

Second, the world economy of 2030 will most certainly not be powered by coal, oil, and natural gas. It is now well accepted that continuing heavy reliance on fossil fuels will cause catastrophic changes in climate. The most recent scientific evidence suggests that stabilizing the climate depends on eventually cutting annual global carbon emissions to some two billion tons per year. about one third the current level. Taking population growth into account, the world in 2030 will therefore have per capita carbon emissions that are one eighth the level of Western Europe today.

The choice then becomes whether to make solar or nuclear power the centrepiece of energy systems. We believe societies will reject nuclear power because of its long list of economic, social, and environmental liabilities. The nuclear industry has been in decline for over a decade. Only ninety-four plants remain under construction, down from nearly 200 a decade ago, and most will be completed in the next few years. Safety concerns and the failure to develop a safe way to store nuclear waste have turned people away from nuclear power.

It is of course possible that scientists could develop new nuclear technologies that are more economical and less accident-prone. Yet this would not solve the waste problem. Nor would it alleviate growing concern about the use of nuclear energy as a stepping stone to developing nuclear weapons. Trying to prevent this in a plutonium-based economy with thousands of operating plants would require a degree of control that is probably incompatible with democratic political systems. Societies are likely to opt instead for diverse, solar-based systems.

The third major assumption is about population size. Current UN projections have the world headed for nearly nine billion people by 2030. This figure implies a doubling or tripling of the populations of Ethiopia, India, Nigeria, and scores of other countries where human numbers are already overtaxing natural support systems. Either these societies will move quickly to encourage smaller families and bring birth rates down, or rising death rates from hunger and malnutrition will check population growth.

The humane path to sustainability by the year 2030 therefore requires a dramatic drop in birth rates. As of 1990, thirteen European countries have stable populations; by 2030, most countries are likely to be in that category. For the world as a whole, human numbers will total well below nine billion. We assume a population of at most eight billion that will either be essentially stable or declining slowly, toward a number the earth can comfortably support indefinitely.

In the end, individual values are what drive social change. Progress towards sustainability thus hinges on a collective deepening of our sense of responsibility to the earth and to future generations. Without a re-evaluation of our personal aspirations and motivations, we will never achieve an environmentally sound global community.

During the seventies and eighties, policymakers assumed that changes in the world energy system would be driven by depletion of the world's fossil fuel resources: as we gradually ran out of oil, coal, and natural gas, we would be forced to develop alternatives. Such a transition would have been comfortably gradual, extending over more than a century. But now the world faces a new set of limits. Long before fossil fuels are exhausted, rising global temperatures from their use could spell an end to civilization as we know it.

The world energy system in the year 2030 is thus likely to bear little resemblance to today's. No longer dominated by fossil fuels, it will be run by solar resources daily replenished by incoming sunlight and by geothermal energy. And it will be far more energy-efficient.

In many ways, the solar age today is where the coal age was when the steam engine was invented in the eighteenth century. At that time, coal was used to heat homes and smelt iron ore, but the notion of using coal-fired steam engines to power factories or transportation systems was just emerging. Yet only a short time later the first railroad started running, and fossil fuels began to transform the world economy.

The late twentieth century, then, is the dawn of the solar age. Many technologies have been developed that allow us to harness the energy of the sun effectively, but these devices are so far only in limited use. Without question, these resources are available in immense quantities: the annual influx of accessible renewable resources in the United States is estimated at 250 times the country's annual use of energy.

The mix of energy sources will likely reflect the climate and natural resources of each particular region. Northern Europe, for example, is likely to rely heavily on wind and hydropower. The economies of northern Africa and the Middle East may instead use direct sunlight. Japan and the Philippines will tap their abundant geothermal energy. And Southeast Asian economies will be powered largely by wood and agricultural wastes, along with sunshine. Some nations, Norway and Brazil for example, already obtain over half their energy from renewables.

Although some countries are likely to import renewable energy, the enormous oil-related bills that characterize modern trade relationships will dwindle. And renewable energy sources are to a large extent inflation-proof: solar, wind, and geothermal power plants require no fuel and so are not vulnerable to fuel price increases.

Due to the abundance of sunlight, direct conversion of solar energy will be the cornerstone of a sustainable world energy system. By 2030, solar panels will heat most residential water around the world. A typical urban landscape will have thousands of collectors sprouting from rooftops, much as television antennas do today.

Solar thermal power is poised to become a principal means of harnessing sunlight. It uses mirrored troughs to focus sunlight onto oil-filled tubes that convey heat to a turbine and generator that then produce electricity. An 80-megawatt solar thermal plant built in the desert east of Los Angeles in 1989 converts an extraordinary twenty-two per cent of the incoming sunlight into electricity; at a third less than the cost of power from new nuclear plants. Such plants may make the deserts of the United States, North Africa, and central Asia major exporters of electricity and hydrogen fuel.

Photovoltaic solar cells are a semi-conductor technology that converts sunlight directly into electricity. Currently, photovoltaic systems are less efficient and four times as expensive as solar thermal power is. But they are already used in remote locations, and the cost is likely to decline rapidly.

Photovoltaics can be used not only in large electricity plants but to power small water pumps and rural communications systems. In addition, all Third World villages can be electrified with this technology. Unlike communities today, these villages will not have to depend on extended power lines connected to centralized plants.

Using this technology, homeowners throughout the world may become producers as well as consumers of electricity. Indeed, photovoltaic shingles have already been developed that allow roofing material itself to become a power source. As costs continue to decline, many homes will be apt to get much of their electricity from photovoltaics, and in sunny regions residents will sell any surplus to the utility company for use by others.

Wind power is an indirect form of solar energy, generated by the sun's differential heating of the earth's atmosphere. Wind energy is already close to competitive with new coal-fired power plants. Engineers are confident that they will soon have improved wind turbines that are economical not just in California's blustery mountain passes, where they are now commonplace, but in vast stretches of the US northern plains and many other areas.

The United States could be deriving ten to twenty per cent of its electricity from the wind by 2030. Wind power is likely to attract new industries into windswept regions. The wind resources of the US Great Plains, which have long pumped water for millions of cattle, may one day be used to generate electricity for sale to Denver, Kansas City, and other major cities.

For hydropower, which now supplies nearly one fifth of the world's electricity, prospects for future growth are most promising in the Third World, where the undeveloped potential is still large. Small-scale projects are likely to be more appealing than the massive projects favoured by governments and international lending agencies in past decades. In deciding which hydropower resources to develop, environmental issues such as land flooding and siltation will play an important role.

Living plants provide another means of capturing solar energy. Through photosynthesis, they convert sunlight into biomass that can be burned. Today, wood already provides twelve per cent of the world's energy, chiefly in the form of firewood and charcoal in developing countries. Its use will surely expand during the next forty years, though resource constraints will not permit it to replace all of the vast quantities of liquid fuels in use today.

One promising approach is to grow energy crops on marginal lands not currently used for food. Land that is to steeply sloping or not sufficiently fertile or well watered for crops might support trees that are periodically harvested. The wood could then be burned directly in a wood-fired power plant or converted to ethanol.

Geothermal energy employs the huge reservoir of heat that lies beneath the earth's surface, making it the only renewable source that does not rely on sunlight. Continuing advances will allow engineers to use previously unexploitable, lower-temperature reservoirs that are hundreds of times as abundant as those in use today. Virtually all Pacific Rim countries, as well as those along East Africa's Great Rift and Mediterranean Sea, are well endowed with geothermal energy.

In both industrial and developing nations, energy production inevitably will be much more decentralized, breaking up the huge industries that have been a dominant part of the economic scene in the late twentieth century.

Getting total global carbon emissions down to two billion tons a year requires vast improvements in energy efficiency. Fortunately, many of the technologies to accomplish such reductions are already at hand and cost-effective. No technical breakthroughs are needed, for example, to double automobile fuel economy, triple the efficiency of lighting systems, or cut typical heating requirements by seventy-five per cent.

Automobiles in 2030 will be apt to get at least 100 miles per gallon of fuel, four times the current average for new cars. A hint of what such vehicles may be like is given in a recently developed prototype, the Volvo LCP 2000. It is an aerodynamic four-passenger car that weighs just half as much as today's models. Moreover, it has a highly efficient and clean-burning diesel engine. With the addition of a continuously variable transmission and a flywheel energy storage device, this vehicle could get ninety miles to the gallon.

Forty years from now, Thomas Edison's revolutionary incandescent light bulbs may be found only in museums, replaced by a variety of new lighting systems, including halogen and sodium lights. The most important new light source may be compact fluorescent bulbs that, for example, use eighteen watts rather than seventy-five to produce the same amount of light.

In 2030, homes are likely to be weather-tight and highly insulated, greatly reducing the need for both heating and cooling.

By the year 2030, a much more diverse set of transportation options will exist. The typical European or Japanese city today has already taken one step toward this future. Highly developed rail and bus systems move people efficiently between home and work: in Tokyo only fifteen per cent of commuters drive cars to the office.

The bicycle will play a major role, as it already does in much of Asia as well as in some industrial-country towns and cities. In Amsterdam and many other communities such as Davis, California, bike-path networks have been developed that encourage widespread use of this form of personal transport. There are already twice as many bikers as cars worldwide. In the bicycle-centred transport system of 2030, the ratio could easily be ten to one.

Forty years from now, people will live closer to their jobs, and much socializing and shopping will be done by bike rather than in a one-ton automobile. Computerized delivery services may allow people to shop from home – consuming less time as well as less energy. In addition, a world that allows only two billion tons of carbon emissions cannot be trucking vast quantities of food and other items thousands of kilometres.

Telecommunications will substitute for travel as well. Many people may work at home or in special satellite offices, connected to colleagues and supervisors by electronic lines rather than crowded highways. Daily trips to the office could be replaced by occasional visits. The saved time and frustration will both raise productivity and the quality of life. The automobile-based modern world is now only about forty years old, but with its damaging air pollution and traffic congestion, it does not represent the pinnacle in human social evolution. Although a world where cars play a minor role may be hard to imagine, our grandparents would have had a hard time visualizing today's world of traffic jams and smog-filled cities.

In the sustainable, efficient economy of 2030, waste reduction and recycling industries will have largely replaced the garbage collection and disposal companies of today. The throwaway society that has emerged during the late twentieth century uses so much energy, emits so much carbon, and generates so much air pollution, and acid rain, water pollution, toxic waste, and rubbish that it is strangling itself. Rooted in planned obsolescence and appeals to convenience, it will be seen by historians as an aberration.

Most materials used today are discarded after one use; roughly two thirds of all aluminium, three quarters of all steel and paper, and an even higher share of plastic. Society will become less energy-intensive and less polluting only if the throwaway mentality is replaced by a recycling ethic.

Just five per cent as much energy is needed to recycle aluminium as to produce it from bauxite ore. For steel produced entirely from scrap, the saving amounts to roughly two thirds. Newsprint from recycled paper takes twenty-five to sixty per cent less energy to make than that from wood pulp. And recycling glass saves up to a third of the energy embodied in the original product.

Recycling is also a key to getting land, air, and water pollution down to acceptable levels. For example, steel produced from scrap reduces air pollution by eighty-five per cent, cuts water pollution by seventy-six per cent, and eliminates mining wastes altogether. Paper from recycled material reduces pollutants entering the air by seventy-four per cent and the water by thirty-five per cent, as well as reducing pressures on forests in direct proportion to the amount recycled.

A hierarchy of options can guide materials policy: the first priority, of course, is to avoid using any nonessential item, a goal that can be furthered by concentrating design talents on durability instead of planned obsolescence. Second is to directly reuse a product, for example, refilling a glass beverage container. The third is to recycle the material to form a new product. Fourth, the material can be burned to exact whatever energy it contains, as long as this can be done safely. And finally, the option of last resort is disposal in a landfill.

For many cities, garbage disposal costs during the last decade increased several-fold, making it cost-effective for them to help establish recycling industries. During the nineties, this trend will be reinforced by the need to reduce carbon emissions, air pollution, acid rain, and toxic waste. In the early stages, countries will move toward comprehensive, systematic recycling of metal, glass, paper, and other materials, beginning with a source separation at the consumer level.

In the sustainable economy of 2030, the principal source of materials for industry will be recycled goods. Most of the raw material for the aluminium mill will come from the local scrap collection centre, not from the bauxite mine. Paper and paper products will be produced at recycling mills, with recycled paper moving through a hierarchy of uses, from high-quality bond to newsprint and, eventually, into cardboard boxes. Industries will turn to virgin raw materials only to replace any losses in use and recycling.

Although early moves away from the throwaway society are concentrating on recycling, sustainability over the long term depends more on eliminating waste flows. One of the most obvious places to reduce the volume of waste generated is in industry, where a restructuring of manufacturing processes can easily slash wastes by a third or more.

Another major potential source of waste reduction lies in the simplification of food packaging. In the United States, consumers spent more on food packaging in 1986 than American farmers earned selling their crops. In the interest of attracting customers, items are sometimes buried in three or four layers of packaging. Forty years from now, government regulation is likely to have eliminated excessive packaging. Throwaway grocery bags will have been replaced by durable, reusable bags of canvas or other material.

Societies in 2030 may also have decided to replace multi-sized and shaped beverage containers with a set of standardized ones made of durable glass that can be reused many times. They could be used for most, if not all, beverages, such as fruit juices, beer, milk, and soda pop. Containers returned to the supermarket or other outlet might become part of an urban or regional computerized inventory.

In addition to recycling and reusing metal, glass, and paper, a sustainable society also recycles nutrients. In nature, one organism's waste is another's sustenance; in urban societies, however, human sewage has become a troublesome source of pollutants in rivers, lakes, and coastal waters. The nutrient in human wastes can be reused safely as long as the process includes measures to prevent the spread of disease.

In some Asian cities, human waste is already systematically returned to the land in vegetable-growing greenbelts around cities. Intensively farmed cropland surrounding some cities there produces vegetables year-round using greenhouses or plastic covering during the winter to extend the growing season. Perhaps the best model is Shanghai: after modestly expanding its urban political boundaries to facilitate sewage recycling, the city now produces an exportable surplus of vegetables.

Some cities will probably find it more efficient to use treated human sewage to fertilize aquacultural operations. A steady flow of nutrients from human waste into ponds can supply food for a vigorously growing population of algae that in turn are consumed by fish. In Calcutta, a sewage-fed aquaculture system now provides 20,000 kilograms of fresh fish each day for sale in the city.

Societies in 2030 will be using the land intensively; the needs of a population more than half again as large as today's cannot be met otherwise. But unlike the present, land use patterns would be abiding by basic principles of biological stability: nutrient retention, carbon balance, soil protection, water conservation, and preservation of species diversity. Harvests will rarely exceed sustainable yields.

Meeting food needs will pose monumental challenges, as some simple numbers illustrate. By 2030, assuming cropland area expands by five per cent between now and then and that population grows to eight billion, cropland per person will have dropped to a third less than we have in today's inadequately fed world. Virtually all of Asia, and especially China, will be struggling to feed its people from a far more meagre cropland area per person.

In light of these constraints, the rural landscapes of 2030 are likely to exhibit greater diversity than they do now. Variations in soils, slope, climate, and water availability will require different patterns and strains of crops grown in different ways so as to maximize sustainable output. For example, farmers may adopt numerous forms of agroforestry; the combined production of crops and trees to provide food, biomass, and fodder, while also adding nutrients to soils and controlling water runoff.

The fundamental changes that are needed in energy, forestry, agriculture, and other physical systems cannot occur without corresponding shifts in the social, economic, and moral character of human societies. During the transition to sustainability, political leaders and citizens alike will be forced to reevaluate their goals and aspirations and to adjust to a new set of principles that have at their core the welfare of future generations.

Shifts in employment will be among the most visible as the transition gets under way. Moving from fossil fuels to a diverse set of renewable energy sources, extracting fewer materials from the earth and recycling more, and revamping farming and forestry practices will greatly expand opportunities in new areas. Losses in coal mining, auto production, and metals prospecting will be offset by gains in the manufacture and sale of photovoltaic solar cells, wind turbines, bicycles, mass transit equipment, and a host of materials recycling technologies.

Wind prospectors, energy efficiency auditors, and solar architects will be among the booming professions stemming from the shift to a highly efficient, renewable energy economy. Numbering in the hundreds of thousands today, jobs in these fields may collectively total in the millions worldwide within a few decades. Opportunities in forestry will expand markedly.

Many people will find their skills valued in new or expanded lines of work. Petroleum geologists may be retrained as geothermal geologists, for example, while traditional midwives continue to broaden their roles to include the spectrum of family planning needs.

Long before 2030, the trend toward ever larger cities and an increasing ratio of urban-to-rural dwellers is likely to have reversed. For example, the increasing energy intensity of food distribution necessitated by cities cannot continue indefinitely. Smaller human settlements will also be favoured by the shift to renewable energy sources.

Power from renewable technologies, whether photovoltaic cells, wood-fired plants, or wind generators, will allow local areas to capitalize on their natural endowments, whether that be strong winds, bright sunshine, abundant woodlands, or proximity to geothermal reservoirs. In so doing, they foster greater local self-reliance.

As the transition to a more environmentally benign economy progresses, sustainability will gradually eclipse growth as the focus of economic policy-making. Over the next few decades, government policies will encourage investments that promote stability and endurance at the expense of those that simply expand short-term production.

As a yardstick of progress, the gross national product (GNP) will be seen as a bankrupt indicator. By measuring flows of goods and services, GNP undervalues qualities a sustainable society strives for, such a durability and resource protection, and over-values planned obsolescence and waste. The pollution caused by a coal-burning power plant, for instance, raises GNP by requiring expenditures on lung disease treatment and the purchase of a scrubber to control emissions. Yet a society would be far better off if power were generated in ways that did not pollute the air in the first place.

In 2030, planners will measure economic and social advances by sustainability criteria rather than simply by growth in short-term output. As economist Herman Daly observes, a new direction of technical progress is needed, 'one that squeezes more service per unit of resource, rather than one that just runs more resources through the system.'

National military budgets in a sustainable world will be a small fraction of what they are today. Moreover, sustainability cannot be achieved without a massive shift of resources from military endeavours into energy efficiency, soil conservation, tree planting, family planning, and other needed development activities. Rather than maintaining large defence establishments, governments may come to rely on a strengthened UN peacekeeping force.

Nations will undoubtedly be co-operating in numerous other ways as well. Careful tracking of changes in atmospheric chemistry, forest cover, land productivity, and ocean resources will be among the many efforts handled by multinational teams of scientists and government workers. Even as individual nations move to decentralize power and decision making within their own borders, they may simultaneously establish an unprecedented degree of co-operation and co-ordination at the international level.

Movement toward a lasting society cannot occur without a transformation of individual priorities and values. Throughout the ages, philosophers and religious leaders have denounced materialism as a viable path to human fulfilment. Yet societies across the ideological spectrum have persisted in equating quality of life with increased consumption.

Because of the strain on resources it creates, materialism simply cannot survive the transition to a sustainable world. As public understanding of the need to adopt simpler and less consumptive life-styles spreads, it will become unfashionable to own fancy new cars and clothes. The potential benefits of unleashing the human energy now devoted to producing, advertising, buying, consuming, and discarding material goods are enormous.

This energy can be channelled into forming richer human relationships, stronger communities, and greater outlets for cultural diversity, music, and the arts. As the amassing of personal and national wealth becomes less of a goal, the gap between haves and have-nots will gradually close.

Follow-up work

The questions arising from Chapter 6 all focus on the necessity for, and nature of, a sustainable society. In particular attention is drawn both to the student's own learning and to consideration of where such issues can be dealt with in different subject areas and interdisciplinary contexts.

1. What are Lester Brown's main arguments for claiming that the transition to a sustainable society is now essential?
2. What are the main assumptions behind this vision of a sustainable future? Would you change any of them?
3. Write your own scenario highlighting the essential features of either energy production or transportation in this sustainable future. Where can these issues be explored in your own subject area or interdisciplinary context?
4. Write your own scenario highlighting the essential features of either waste management or land use in this sustainable future. Where can these issues be explored in your own subject area or interdisciplinary context?
5. What organisations within the local, national and global community are working towards such a future? How can you incorporate examples of their vision, work and experience, into your own teaching?

Chapter 7

SOME EXEMPLAR ACTIVITIES

David Hicks

The activities in this chapter provide a variety of ways for students to begin exploring the future. Each activity follows the same format and is intended for use with students and/or colleagues. Whilst each can stand alone they will be most effective if used as part of a more extensive study of futures or other related issues. An extended repertoire of such activities for classroom use can be found in Hicks, D. *Educating for the Future: A Practical Classroom Guide,* World Wide Fund for Nature, 1994. Permission will need to be requested from the publisher to photocopy Activity Sheets referred to below.

Trends for the future

Purpose
To introduce students to some key global trends that are likely to affect their lives now and in the 21st century.

Preparation
Each pair of participants needs a set of the nine statements entitled 'Some trends for the future' cut up into slips (Activity Sheet 7.1). At the end of the activity each person can be given a copy of the complete sheet. Time needed 35–45 minutes.

Procedure
* Students sit in pairs with a space between them on which to work. Each pair is given a set of 'Some trends for the future' cut up into a series of 9 slips. The task is for each pair to agree on a diamond ranking of these slips in response to the question 'Which of these trends do you think will have the most significant impact on the future?'

* Since partners have to *agree* on their ranking they will need to discuss both their individual responses to the trends and their criteria for defining 'most significant'. No further guidance need be given since one purpose of this activity is to encourage students to formulate their own responses to the material. It is useful to move around the group to 'tune-in' to the on-going discussion. Occasional prompts may be useful to broaden the scope of discussion.

* After 20 minutes one person from each pair reports briefly to the whole group on their 'top 3' trends. Why did they select these three? What is so important about them? What evidence do *they* have for these trends? What trends have been left out? What sense of the future does the group seem to have?

* Any of these trends could be a subject for subsequent research. Several are taken from Naisbitt, J. & Aburdene, P. *Megatrends 2000*, Pan, 1991. Their analysis of such trends is, however, often both shallow and ethnocentric. Another source is Brown, L., Flavin, C., & Kane, H. *Vital Signs: The Trends That Are Shaping Our Future 1992–1993*, Earthscan Publications, 1992.

Activity Sheet 7.1

Some trends for the future

Cultural diversity
Whilst we are now all part of one global system, it is ethnic, cultural and historical differences amongst peoples that will increasingly influence national and global affairs in the future.

The Pacific rim
The centre of world trade is now shifting from the Atlantic to the Pacific rim. Asian countries bordering the Pacific will become more important as they undergo the fastest period of economic expansion in history.

Women in leadership
Women are now increasingly taking up leadership roles in business, especially in the U.S. This trend is likely to spread and will have a significant impact on the way in which business is organised in the future.

Biotechnology
The new scientific frontier of genetic engineering is about to transform our lives whether we like it or not. This includes both the creation of new plant and animal breeds as well as alteration of human genes.

Religious revival
There are now clear signs of a worldwide religious and spiritual revival, ranging from growth of fundamentalist and evangelical groups to the spread of New Age beliefs and a renaissance of more ancient traditions.

Environmental concern
Due to issues such as global warming and ozone depletion there is now an upsurge of popular interest in environmental issues. Increasingly people are aware of the need to preserve and nurture the planet itself.

Wealth and poverty
The nature of the world economic system is such that the gap between the countries of the Rich North and the Poor South will continue to increase. This growing division will create serious future problems.

Changing worldviews
In the West there is now a major value shift away from a predominantly scientific and mechanistic view of the world to a more holistic and ecological one. This can now be seen in many fields of enquiry.

Trend X
One of the most important trends in the last decade of the twentieth century which will have a major impact on the future is . . .

Global timelines

Purpose
For students to explore the differences between their probable and preferable futures for the planet.

Preparation
Each pair needs a sheet of A3 paper and an assortment of coloured pens. Time needed 45–60 minutes.

Procedure
* Students work in pairs to draw their own probable and preferable future timelines under the heading 'Britain in the world, the world in Britain.' Probable futures are all those we *expect* to come about. Preferable futures are all those we think *ought* to come about.

* The heading is intended to remind students that Britain has both many links *out* to the rest of the world and also that the rest of the world is present *within* Britain in a multiplicity of ways. On the left-hand side of the timeline important post-war events and trends should be indicated in as graphic and eye-catching a way as possible.

* Students then mark on their probable timeline, as graphically as possible, the events and trends that they *expect* to occur within the next fifty years. Finally students mark on their preferable timeline the events and trends that they would *like* to come about within the next fifty years.

* Completed timelines should be displayed and the whole group given time to study these. Depending on the size of the group all or some pairs then make brief reports on their timelines. Whole group discussion should then focus on questions such as: What are the main similarities/differences between their probable futures? What are the main similarities and differences between their preferable futures? What are the main differences between the two? How might the expected probable futures affect the lives of the children they will teach? What action is needed to bring such preferable futures about? What organisations are already working towards such futures? How might such timelines drawn by children vary depending on age, gender, class and ethnicity.?

Preferable futures

Purpose
To highlight the importance of exploring preferable futures, particularly in relation to issues of justice and sustainability.

Preparation
Participants will need copies of the Activity Sheet 7.2 'Goals for a better world.' Time needed c. 90 minutes.

Procedure
* Students look again at the preferable part of their global timelines. Small groups are formed by three pairs coming together. They take it in turns to share the following: a) what is the most *important* feature of your preferable timeline? b) what key areas of concern does it particularly cover, e.g. the environment, work, health etc?

* Each group then works to create a composite picture of their preferred future. This should be in both graphic and written form. Each group summarises the main features of their collective prefer-

able future to the whole group. They highlight any elements which they feel may act as 'new guiding images' for society.

* Students then look at copies of 'Goals for a better world' (Activity Sheet 7.2). The group takes each goal in turn and considers what it would look like in practice, locally and globally, by discussing the following questions. Alternatively each group could look at *one* goal.

1. *Why* is this a critical goal for a better world?
2. What might it *look like* in practice?
3. What is *already* being done to achieve such goals and by whom?

* Groups report back by displaying their answers as a checklist or flowchart. Further discussion can centre around questions such as: What might we want to do to help achieve such goals? How might these goals be perceived differently depending, for example, on gender, age or ethnicity?

Activity Sheet 7.2

Goals for a better world

1. Economic welfare
Everyone should have access to the basic necessities of life such as food, clothes, shelter, health care and education. There should be both a minimum level of welfare, below which no one should drop, but also a maximum level beyond which no one should go, due to the finite nature of many of the earth's resources.

2. Freedom from violence
No one should be subjected to direct personal violence, e.g. through assault, robbery or war and neither should they suffer from indirect violence. Unjust social, political and economic systems can equally cause suffering in the form of poverty, hunger, and other deprivation.

3. Social justice
What one 'has' should not depend on who one 'is' in society. Thus the practices and procedures for allocating resources should not discriminate, directly or indirectly, on the basis of gender, race, class, culture or group.

4. Ecological diversity
This requires full and appropriate protection of the biosphere on which all life depends. Thus the right of non-human species must also be recognised and the need for concerned stewardship of air, water, soil, creatures and plants.

5. Participation in decisions
Genuine participation in all aspects of one's life offers opportunities for responsibility, personal growth and enrichment. It means being in control of one's own life choices and being free to choose. This leads to ownership of decisions and is the reverse of alienation.

Futures thinking

Purpose
To relate a range of futures ideas to current classroom practice.

Preparation
Each person needs a copy of Activity Sheet 7.3 'Futures thinking: some examples.'

Procedure
* Students work in small groups of 5 or 6 to consider the checklist entitled 'Futures thinking' which highlights some of the main elements of a futures perspective in the curriculum. The group selects examples of futures thinking which can be applied to either a particular issue or a specific National Curriculum requirement or cross-curricular theme.

* How does each example of futures thinking enhance the study of that issue or the particular curriculum area in question? A spokesperson should report back briefly from each group. Whole-group discussion should then focus on the question 'Why is a

futures perspective an essential element of the curriculum in the 1990s?'

Activity Sheet 7.3

Futures thinking: some examples

1. State of the planet
In the last decade of the 20th century the state of the planet continues to give serious cause for concern. Issues to do with the environment, development, conflict and human rights, have a major impact both locally and globally. Students need to know about the causes of global problems, their likely impact on the future and the action needed to help resolve them.

2. Managing change
In periods of rapid social and technological change the past cannot provide an accurate guide to the future. Anticipation and adaptability, foresight and flexibility, innovation and intuition, become increasingly essential tools for survival. Students need to develop such skills in order to become more adaptable and pro-active towards change.

3. Hopes and fears
Hopes and fears for the future often influence decision making in the present. Fears can lead to the avoidance of problems rather than their resolution. Clarifying hopes for the future often enhances motivation in the present and thus positive action for change. Students need to explore their own hopes and fears for the future and learn to work creatively with them.

4. Views of the future
People's views of the future may vary greatly depending, for example, on status, age, gender and culture, as well as their attitudes to change, to the environment and technology. Students need to be aware of how views of the future thus differ and the ways in which this affects people's priorities in the present.

5. Alternative futures
At any point in time a range of different futures is possible. It is useful to distinguish between probable futures, those which seem *likely* to come about, and preferable futures, those we feel *should* come about. Students need to explore and debate a range of probable and preferable futures, from the personal to the global.

6. Past/present/future
Interdependence exists across both space and time. Past, present and future are inextricably connected. We are directly linked back in time by the oldest members of the community and forward nearly a century by those born today. Students need to explore these links and to gain a sense of both continuity and change as well as of responsibility for the future.

7. Visions for the future
The transition from one century to another, and particularly from one millennium to another, is often seen as a turning point for society. What needs to be left behind and what taken forward? Visions of a better future can help to motivate active and responsible citizenship in the present. Students therefore need to develop their own skills of envisioning and their use of the creative imagination.

8. Future generations
Economists, philosophers and international lawyers increasingly recognise the rights of future generations. It has been suggested that no generation should inherit *less* human and natural wealth than the one that preceded it. Students need to discuss the rights of future generations and what the responsibility to uphold them may involve.

9. Sustainable futures
Current consumerist lifestyles on this planet are increasingly seen as unsustainable often causing more damage than benefit. Sustainable development, on the other hand, prioritises concern for the environment, the poorest members of the community, and the needs of future generations. Students need to understand how this applies to their everyday lives both personally and professionally.

Sustainable futures

Purpose
To provide an introduction to some key elements of a sustainable future.

Preparation
Each pair of students will need copies of Activity Sheet 7.4 'Notes on Sustainability' cut up into slips. Time needed about one hour.

Procedure
* Sustainable development has been most succinctly defined as 'development which meets the needs of the present without jeopardising the needs of future generations.' Participants work in pairs with a clear space between them. They lay out the statements from 'Notes on sustainability' (Activity Sheet 7.4) to create their own annotated flow diagram (on a sheet of A3 paper) to show how each of these elements are interrelated. Around each statement they write a) examples we know about; b) things we want to research. These are then displayed and all or selected flow diagrams spoken to.

* Subsequently students work in small groups. Each group selects one element of sustainability to apply either to a particular environmental or development issue or a specific area of the curriculum. What does the notion of sustainability add to the study of that issue or curriculum area? A spokesperson should report back briefly from each group. The session concludes with whole-group discussion on 'Why an understanding of sustainability is an essential element in education for responsible citizenship.

* Additional research on sustainability could initially refer to the sources used to compile these 'notes'. They were:

Brown, L. et al. *State of the World 1992*, Earthscan Publications, London, 1992
Brown, L., Flavin, C. & Postel, S. *Saving the Planet: How to Shape an Environmentally Sustainable Global Economy*, W. W. Norton & Co., New York, 1991
Green justice: the South speaks out, *The New Internationalist*, No. 230, April 1992
Milbrath, L. *Envisioning a Sustainable Society*, State University of New York Press, Albany, 1989
Meadows, D. & D. *Beyond the Limits: Global Collapse or Sustainable Future*, Earthscan Publications, London, 1992.

Activity Sheet 7.4

Notes on Sustainability

Energy

Continued reliance on fossil fuels such as coal and oil is likely to cause major climatic change, whilst nuclear power has increasingly proved to be a social, economic and environmental liability. A sustainable future will emphasise greatly increased energy efficiency together with renewable energy sources such as solar, wind, water and biomass.

Transport

Unrestricted use of the car has created a major series of related problems ranging from severe traffic congestion and dangerous air pollution to urban sprawl. A sustainable future will minimise the need for people to travel, with jobs being closer to home, and emphasise the use of public transport, buses, trams and light rail, as well as cycling and walking.

Environment

Unrestrained consumption of the earth's resources is beginning to produce irreversible damage to the biosphere and a major loss of biodiversity, on land, air and water. In a sustainable future people will see themselves as a part of nature rather than separate from it and environmental conservation will have as high a priority as economic growth.

Economics

Traditional models of development focus narrowly on economic growth as the indicator of 'progress'. A range of costs are thus 'discounted' e.g. damage to the environment, the effect on the poor, and the effect on future generations. In a sustainable future much more comprehensive indicators of human well-being will be used.

Cities

Uncontrolled urban growth is having a profound impact on human and planetary well-being, both in the rich and poor world.

In a sustainable future planning will be more participatory and land-use and transport policies carefully integrated. Homes, jobs, services and amenities will be mixed together and thus more easily accessible by public transport, cycle or foot.

Poverty
In the poor South $^3/_4$ of the world's people consume 17% of the world's resources, whilst in the rich North $^1/_4$ of the world's people consume 83% of the resources. Debt and falling export prices encourage unsustainable development. A sustainable future for all requires a major change of direction in the policies and lifestyles of the North towards greater justice and equity.

Resources
In a sustainable future waste reduction and recycling will have replaced rubbish collection and disposal. Planned obsolescence, appeals to convenience, and the throwaway society of today will be seen as an aberration. Manufacturing will thus be less energy intensive and less polluting. Many items will be re-used, recycled to form new products or burnt to extract energy.

Farming
Current intensive farming methods often lead to extensive land degradation and a massive international effort is needed to protect soil, conserve water and restore soil productivity. In a sustainable future more emphasis will be placed on organic husbandry and mixed farming with biological pest controls. More food will be grown and consumed locally and regionally.

Population
During the last decade of this century world population is expected to increase by at least 960 million people. The rate of population growth tends to fall as standards of living, health and education, especially of women, increase. In a sustainable future due emphasis will be given to this and world population could stabilise at eight billion by the year 2030.

Envisioning the future – Elise Boulding

Purpose
To enable students to visualise elements of their preferred future through use of the creative imagination.

Preparation
The reader needs to be familiar with the text. A3 paper and pens. Time needed c. 3 hours.

Procedure

1. The goal statement: checking out your own hopes for the world
State one or more particular sociocultural/institutional achievements in relation to the overall goal of a more just and sustainable future that you, bringing your own expertise to bear in the most hopeful and optimistic vein that you can draw on, would like to see realized three decades from now, in 20—.

A. On completion of this exercise, members of the group will briefly share out loud some of their goal statements. If there is time, this can be done in 3-person groups.

B. Now, after this brief discussion, reread your own goal statement and then rewrite, edit, or modify that statement in any way you wish. As the workshop proceeds, you are always free to go back and improve upon your initial goal statement.

2. Exercising the imagination: memories
We are going to enter the world 20— through the door of our imagination in a few minutes. First we need to get into the imagining mode. To do this each of us will enter our personal memory world and pick one memory to reexperience. It may be from our recent or long-ago past. It should be 'good' memory, one you will enjoy reliving. You will be able to describe in detail the setting; the people involved; and the smells, sights, sounds, and feel of the place. The longer you explore the memory, the more you will see. Make some notes about the memory so you do not forget the details. In a few minutes you will divide into pairs and tell each other these memories.

3. Moving into the future

Now we are almost ready to step into the world of 20—. To do this we will pass through an opening – whatever opening we can find once we have stepped mentally outside this building. We will keep our minds tuned to the remembering mode, only now we are asked to remember the future. How will we do this? Know that everything each of us has ever experienced, seen, heard, tasted, touched, thought, felt, from our time in the womb to the present, is encoded in some manner in our being. This record of our total life experience is not available to our conscious analytical mind except in fragments at certain moments. When we fantasize, however, that whole repository is opened up and contributes, in ways we do not consciously design, to that which we fantasize. What you are now being asked to do is focused fantasizing, or imagining. It is focused because you are bringing intentionality to it. Remember your hopes for the world in 20—. Then allow your fantasizing mind to draw on your own rich storehouse of experience to construct/remember a world in which these hopes have been realized. You are not producing or creating a model world in an analytical sense. In terms of your conscious mind you are stepping into 20— as an observer, looking to see what you can find there. Your fantasizing/imagining capacity will do the rest. Do not try to analyze what you see. That comes later. Now you are looking, recording.

It's all right to ask questions, however, in order to see more clearly. It's all right to let your imagination move you around in 20— to get a better view, to see more things. You are watching a movie unreeling in your head, so to speak, only unlike the movie-watching situation you can question the characters.

You want to look for specifics. You have brought your hopes with you. Look to see what is happening in concrete instances in specific arenas of life. Look for demonstrations that this world of 20— actually represents a way of life that incorporates your goals of 30 years ago. What are people doing – the children, the elderly, the middle-years folk, the men, the women? What kind of household groupings do you find, what kinds of buildings? What is the physical environment like? Can you identify neighbourhoods? Are there cities? What kinds of occupations do you see people following? Can you tell how decisions about the polity are made, or how people travel and make connections across distances. How do people of different ages learn new things? How are conflicts and differences handled, both the local conflicts and the far-away ones? Do you see anyone playing? How do they play? Do you see anything that might correspond to the churches of 30 years ago.?

Some people will actually see the equivalent of a movie unreeling in their heads. Others only see disconnected image fragments, momentary flashes of individual scenes. Still others will not experience the future visually, but through other senses, other modes of representation. However you arrive at your perceptions, record what you experience. There is no one 'right way' of imagining. Make notes and sketches about what you see.

(*Note*: Because some people have more difficulty than others in moving into the future in the imagination, the group will step into the future for a brief exploratory survey, then come back to 19— to discuss what people saw, how difficulties were overcome, and so forth. With the second return to 20—, you will be left free to explore. *However*, a few may have continuing difficulty with getting into the future. Please feel free to come to the facilitator and discuss how to deal with this. A compromise solution for handling this exercise may be to make up a story. Please do not do this, however, without discussing it with the facilitator first.)

4. Clarification

What you have seen will become clearer as you tell it to others. Try mentally to stay in 20—, and describe what is going on to your partners in the groups of three you will now form. Listen carefully to each other, and ask questions of each other. The questioning is for clarification only. What each of you has seen has its own quality of viridity. It is important to respect each other's images and the values that lie behind them. Through questioning and clarification, each of you will understand more fully what you have seen. Just as in your childhood remembering, a question can send you back to look again, and you will see more than you saw at first. You will keep adding to the richness of your seeing; you will continue to discover new details, new aspects. Make notes about your further insights into your own imagery of 20—.

5. Consequence mapping and world construction

A. Staying in the same group of three, now begin to ask more analytical questions of your imaging material. What kind of world is out there? Refer back to your goal statement for a theme to 'build' your world around. Draw on each other's future memories to the extent you wish to. For the purposes of this exercise, you are still in 20—. Speak of 20— as the present. If you wish to refer to 19—, do so in the past tense. Decide what structures must exist in this world you are in to account for what you have seen. How is family life organized? What are the economic and political systems? How is education organized? How does civic and cultural life maintain itself? What makes this society tick? Account for your society locally, and move as far out as you can in terms of regions and the planet as a whole. Are there nation-states?

Time will be a limiting factor here, so begin with those aspects of the society that interest you most. You can add others later (even after this workshop is over). Take turns helping each other analyze the structure of the world you have each seen individually. On the basis of this analysis, each of you will draw a visual or diagrammatic representation of what you know about that world, on the paper that will be provided.

B. The next stage is for all participants to hold their paper up so others can see it, and to begin moving around to inspect each other's depictions of 20—. Form groups of five on the basis of some degree of theme compatibility. Each team of five will now construct a common world, based on its members' individual depictions. Deal with contradictions and discrepancies between views as best you can, and produce a visual representation of that common world on paper. Remember, you are still in 20—. That is your 'present' during the whole exercise. Each team of five will then give a brief explanation of its world to the assembled workshop.

6. The future's history

You are still in 20—. Working individually again, step back into your fantasizing mode and begin to reminisce about how all this came about. It is important that you do this reminiscing from the future-present moment of 20—. Like historians of the real past, you will work with fragments of 'information' and weave them into a plausible story. Your fragments will come to you in the same way that the images of 20— came to you, culled by your fantasy from your own life-experience repository. Begin with 'last year'. What happened that year to bring about the world of 20—?

Then go back in five-year intervals, ending with the 'real' present. While it is important to go back from the future, you will not always be sure in what year something happened (that is true of the real past, too). In that case, jot the happening down in the margins and then insert it when you are clearer about the order in which things happened. Indicate a crucial turning-point year if you can. (When time allows, this future-remembering exercise should be repeated with your world-construction team, to create collective memories.)

7. Action planning in the present

Working individually again, think through what you as an individual might do now, this year, to help bring about this future world you have experienced in imagination. First think about the action settings available to you. List them: your family, neighbourhood, community settings, workplace, organizations you are involved in, where you shop, and so forth.

Now, what objectives might you set for yourself – concrete, specific goals that you could achieve in the short term, that is, in the coming months? Who will your allies be? How will you relate to decision makers? Now begin to flesh out one project, based on your answers to these questions. (When time allows, this action exercise should be repeated with your world-construction team to create collective action plans.)

Note

This chapter particularly draws on work done with John Fien at Griffith University, Brisbane, for the Environmental and Development Education Project for Teacher Education of the Australian Association for Environmental Education.

NOTES ON CONTRIBUTORS

Elise Boulding, Professor Emerita of Sociology at Dartmouth College, now lives in Boulder, Colorado – where she heads the University of Colorado-based IPRA Commission on Peace Building in the Middle East. Active in the peace research community since the 1950s, she has also written extensively on women's roles and in the field of futures studies. Her most recent book was *Building a Global Civic Culture: Education for an Interdependent World* (Teachers College Press, 1988).

Lester Brown is Director of the prestigious Worldwatch Institute in Washington, which produces the annual *State of the World* report, translated into nearly 30 languages. He is one of the world's leading experts on the global issues relating to sustainable development. He is a recipient of the MacArthur Foundation 'genius award' and winner of the UN's 1989 environment prize.

Richard A. Slaughter is Lecturer in Futures and Social Policy at the Institute of Education, University of Melbourne, Australia. He is a prolific and influential writer in the field of futures education and an Associate Editor of the journal *Futures*. His most recent publication, with ***Headley Beare***, is *Education for the 21st Century*, published by Routledge in 1992.

ABOUT THE EDITOR

David Hicks is Director of the Global Futures Project based at Bath College of Higher Education in the UK. From 1980–89 he directed the innovative World Studies 8–13 Project and is a leading expert on both global education and futures education. He has worked extensively with teachers in the UK, Italy, Canada, and Australia. He is particularly interested in working with groups on 'envisioning the future'.

Acknowledgements

Chapter 2 Adapted from Hicks, D. 'Reclaiming the future: what every educator needs to know,' keynote lecture given to the Australian Association for Environmental Education, September 1992

Chapter 3 Adapted from Hicks, D. 'Preparing for the millennium: reflections on the need for futures education,' *Futures*, 23 (6), 1991

Chapter 4 Slaughter, R. 'Changing images of futures in the 20th century,' *Futures*, 23 (5), 1991

Chapter 5 Boulding, E. 'Image and action in peace building,' *Journal of Social Issues*, 44 (2), 1988

Chapter 6 Brown, L. 'A sustainable future,' *Resurgence*, No. 147, July/August 1991

Chapter 7 The procedure for Envisioning the Future is taken

from Appendix 2 of Boulding, E. *Building a Global Civic Culture: Education for an Interdependent World*, Teachers College Press, New York, 1988.

REFERENCES

Chapter 1

1. Postel, S. Chapter 1 in *State of the World 1992*, Brown, L. et al., ed., Earthscan Publications, 1992.
2. A good example of the theoretical and practical debates surrounding the liberal and reconstructionist traditions can be found in Richardson, R. *Daring to be a Teacher: Essays, Stories and Memoranda*, Trentham Books, 1990.
3. See for example Huckle, J. *What we Consume*, ten curriculum units on issues of environment and development, World Wide Fund for Nature, 1988/92; also Fien, J. *Education for the Environment: Critical Curriculum Theorizing and Environmental Education*, Faculty of Environmental Sciences, Griffith University, Brisbane, 1992.
4. Brown, L., Flavin, C. & Kane, H. *Vital Signs: The Trends That Are Shaping Our Future 1993–94*, Earthscan Publications, 1993.
5. Slaughter, R. *The Foresight Principle: Cultural recovery in the 21st Century*, Adamantine Press, 1994.
6. See Hicks, D. *Educating for the Future: A Practical Classroom Guide*, World Wide Fund for Nature UK, 1993: also Beare, H. & Slaughter, R. *Education for the 21st Century*, Routledge, 1992. On futures see Lloyd, B. ed. *Framing the Future: a 21st Century Reader*, Adamantine Press, 1994; the journal *Futures* is available from Turpin Distribution Services Ltd., Blackhorse Road, Letchworth, Herts SG6 1HN.

7. *Curriculum Guidance 3: The Whole Curriculum*, National Curriculum Council, York, 1990.

Chapter 2

1. 'Earth's future in the balance, say top scientists,' *The Guardian*, 27th February 1992.
2. Meadows, D. & D., Randers, J. *Beyond the Limits: Global Collapse or a Sustainable Future*, Earthscan Publications, London, 1992.
3. Toffler, A. *Learning for Tomorrow: The Role of the Future in Education*, Vintage Books/Random House, New York, 1974.
4. *Young Eyes: Children's Visions of the Future Environment*, A report commissioned by BT, Henley Centre for Forecasting, London, 1991.
5. Slaughter, R. *What Do We Do Now The Future Is Here?* University of Lancaster, 1985. (Out of print)
6. Naisbitt, J. & Aburdene, P. *Megatrends 2000*, Pan Books, London, 1991.
7. Wagar, Warren W. *The Next Three Futures: Paradigms of Things to Come*, Adamantine Press, London, 1992; Marien, M. & Jennings, L. *What I Have Learned: Thinking About the Future Then and Now*, Greenwood Press, Westport, Connecticut, 1987.
8. *Futures*, Butterworth-Heinemann, Oxford (available from Turpin Distribution Services Ltd, Blackhorse Road, Letchworth, Herts SG6 1HN, UK); *Futures Research Quarterly*, World Future Society, 7910 Woodmont Avenue, Suite 450, Bethesda, MD 20814–6089, USA.
9. Slaughter, R. 'Changing images of futures in the 20th century,' *Futures*, 23 (5), 1991; pp. 499–515.
10. Polak, F. *The Image of the Future*, translated by Elise Boulding, Jossy Bass/Elsevier, San Francisco, 1972.
11. Quoted in Hicks, D. & Steiner, M. *Making Global Connections: A World Studies Workbook*, Oliver & Boyd/Longman, Harlow, 1989; p. 10.
12. Ziegler, W. *Envisioning the Future: A Mindbook of Exercises for Future-Inventors*, Futures-Invention Associates, Denver, CO, 1989.
13. See chapter 6, Uses of the Imagination, in Boulding, E. *Building a Global Civic Culture: Education for an Interdependent World*, Teachers College Press, NY, 1988.
14. Boulding, E. Image and action in peace building,' *Journal of Social Issues*, 44 (2), 1988; pp. 17–37.
15. Macy, J. *World as Lover, World as Self*, Parallax Press, Berkeley, CA, 1991.
16. Kumar, K. *Utopianism*, Open University Press, Milton Keynes, 1991.
17. Yothu Yindi, *Tribal Voice*, from a track called 'Treaty,' Mushroom Records, 1992.
18. Galeano, E. *The Book of Embraces*, W. W. Norton & Co, NY, 1991.
19. Shiva, V. *Staying Alive: Women, Ecology and Development*, Zed Books, London, 1989.
20. Masini, E. 'Women as builders of the future,' *Futures*, August 1987; pages 431–36.
21. Brown, L. et al. *State of the World 1992*, Earthscan Publications, London, 1992; p. 5.
22. Milbrath, L. *Envisioning a Sustainable Society: Learning Our Way Out*, State University of New York Press, Albany, 1989.

23. Richardson, R. *Daring to be a Teacher: Essays, Stories, Memoranda*, Trentham Books, Stoke-on-Trent, 1990.
24. Huckle, J. Environmental Education, chapter 10 in *The New Social Curriculum: A Guide to Cross-Curricular Issues*, Dufour, B. ed., Cambridge University Press, 1990.
25. See Meadows 2 above, p. 230.

Chapter 3

1. *Curriculum Guidance 3: The Whole Curriculum* (York, National Curriculum Council, 1990), page 1.
2. See also N. Gough, 'An accidental astronaut: learning with science fiction', in G. Willis and W. Schubert (editors), *Reflections from the Heart of Curriculum Inquiry: Understanding Curriculum and Teaching Through the Arts* (Albany, NY, State University of New York, 1991).
3. D. Hicks, 'Lessons from global education: avoiding a nationalistic curriculum', *Education 3–13, 18* (3), 1990, pages 39–45.
4. For details write to: Birmingham Development Education Centre, Selly Oak Colleges, Bristol Road, Birmingham B29 6LE, UK; Manchester Development Education Project, c/o Manchester Metropolitan University, 801 Wilmslow Road, Manchester M20 0SC, UK.
5. World Studies 8–13 Project, School of Education, Manchester Metropolitan University, 799 Wilmslow Road, Manchester M20 8RR, UK.
6. I. Lister, 'Global and international approaches in political education', in C. Harber (editor), *Political Education in Britain* (Lewes, UK, Falmer Press, 1987), pages 47–62.
7. See for example, D. Hicks and M. Steiner (editors), *Making Global Connections: A World Studies Workbook* (Edinburgh, Oliver and Boyd, 1989), pages 26–27; and G. Pike and D. Selby, *Global Teacher, Global Learner* (London, Hodder and Stoughton, 1987), pages 12–21 and 151–164.
8. R. Richardson, *Daring to be a Teacher: Essays, Stories and Memoranda* (Stoke-on-Trent, UK, Trentham Books, 1989), page 7.
9. A. Toffler, *Future Shock* (New York, Bantam, 1971); D. H. Meadows et al, *The Limits to Growth* (London, Earth Island Ltd. 1972); Toffler, *op cit*, reference 2; N. Cross *et al, Designing the Future* (Milton Keynes, Open University Press, 1975).
10. D. Hicks, 'World Studies 8–13: a short history 1980–89', *Westminster Studies in Education, 13*, 1990, pages 61–80.
11. R. M. Fitch and and C. R. Svengalis, *Futures Unlimited: Teaching About Worlds to Come*, Bulletin 59 (Washington, DC, National Council for the Social Studies, 1979).
12. R. Slaughter, 'Probing beneath the surface: review of a decade's futures work', *Futures, 21(5)*, October 1989, pages 447–465.
13. S. Fisher and D. Hicks, *World Studies 8–13: A Teacher's Handbook* (Edinburgh, Oliver and Boyd, 1985), pages 132–160.
14. N. Gough, 'Alternative futures in geographical education', in J. Fien and R. Gerber (editors), *Teaching Geography for a Better World* (Edinburgh, Oliver and Boyd, 1988), pages 164–180.
15. N. Gough, 'Futures in Australian education: tacit, token and taken for granted', *Futures, 22(3)*, April 1990, pages 298–310.
16. Fisher and Hicks, *op cit*, reference 15; Pike and Selby, *op cit*, reference 9.

17. R. Slaughter, 'Futures', in D. Hicks (editor), *Education for Peace: Issues, Principles and Practice in the Classroom* (London, Routledge, 1988), pages 214–228; Gough, *op cit*, reference 16.
18. R. Slaughter, *Futures Tools and Techniques* (Melbourne, Future Studies Centre, 1987); R. Slaughter (editor), *Studying the Future* (Canberra, Commission for the Future and Australian Bicentennial Authority, 1989).
19. C. E. and H. F. Whaley, *Future Images: Future Studies for Grades 4 to 12* (New York, Trillium Press, 1986).
20. L. R. Beres and H. R. Targ, *Constructing Alternative World Futures: Re-ordering the Planet* (Cambridge, MA, Schenkman Publishing Company, 1977), pages 9–23 and 63–91.
21. C. Freeman and M. Jahoda, *World Futures: The Great Debate* (Oxford, Martin Robertson, 1978).
22. J. Robertson, *The Sane Alternative: A Choice of Futures* (The Old Bakehouse, Cholsey, Wallingford, Oxon OX10 9NU, UK, 1983).
23. M. Marien and L. Jennings (editors), *What I Have Learnt: Thinking About the Future Then and Now* (New York, Greenwood Press, 1987).
24. J. Coates and J. Jarratt, *What Futurists Believe* (Bethesda, MD, World Future Society, 1989).
25. J. Naisbitt and P. Aburdene, *Megatrends 2000* (London, Pan Books, 1991); F. Kinsman, *Millennium: Towards Tomorrow's Society* (London, Penguin Books, 1991); A. Toffler, *Powershift: Knowledge, Wealth, and Violence at the Edge of the 21st Century* (New York, Bantam Books, 1990).
26. D. Hicks, *Educating for the Future: A Practical Classroom Guide*, World Wide Fund for Nature UK, 1994.
27. See, for example, R. B. J. Walker, *One World, Many Worlds: Struggles for a Just World Peace* (London, Zed Books, 1988).
28. See for example special issue on 'Gender and change', *Futures, 21*(1), February 1989; V. Shiva, *Staying Alive: Women, Ecology and Development* (London, Zed Books, 1989); I. Diamond and G. F. Orenstein (editors), *Reweaving the World: The Emergence of Ecofeminism* (San Francisco, CA, Sierra Club Books, 1990); and N. B. Albinski, *Women's Utopias in British and American Fiction* (London, Routledge, 1988).
29. See, for example, E. B. Weiss, *In Fairness to Future Generations: International Law, Common Patrimony and Intergenerational Equity* (New York, Transnational Publishers, 1989).
30. See, for example, W. Ziegler, *Designing and Facilitating Projects and Workshops in Futures-Invention* (Denver, CO, Futures-Invention Associates, 1987); E. Boulding, 'Image and action in peace building', *Journal of Social Issues, 44*(2), 1988, pages 17–37; and J. Macy, *World as Lover, World as Self* (San Francisco, CA, Parallax Press, 1991).
31. See, for example, L. Milbrath, *Envisioning a Sustainable Society: Learning the Way Out* (Albany, NY, State University of New York Press, 1989).
32. See, for example, B. Goodwin and K. Taylor, *The Politics of Utopia: A Study in Theory and Practice* (London, Hutchinson, 1982); and K. Kumar, *Utopianism* (Milton Keynes, Open University Press, 1991).
33. S. Coleman and P. O'Sullivan (editors), *William Morris and News From Nowhere: A Vision for Our Time* (Bideford, UK, Green Books, 1990), page 9.
34. William Morris, quoted in *ibid*, page 28.

Chapter 4

1. Sir Karl Popper speaking at the World Congress of Philosophy, Brighton, UK, 1988.
2. B. J. Huber, 'Images of the future', in J. Fowles (editor), *Handbook of Futures Research* (Greenwood Press, New York, 1978), pages 179–224.
3. For a delightful insight into this theme, see 'How expositions expose themselves', in U. Eco *Travels in Hyperreality* (London, Picador, 1986), pages 296–299.
4. E. M. Forster, 'The machine stops', in *The Eternal Moment and Other Stories* (London, HBJ, 1929).
5. D. Dunphy, *The Challenge of Change* (Melbourne, Australian Broadcasting Commission, 1972), page 19.
6. I. Mitroff and W. Bennis, *The Unreality Industry* (New York, Carol Publishing Group, 1989).
7. See F. Polak, *The Image of the Future*, translated by Elise Boulding, (New York, Oceana, 1961).
8. See R. Slaughter, 'Probing beneath the surface: review of a decade's futures work', *Futures 21(5)*, 1989, pages 447–465.
9. See R. Slaughter, 'The machine at the heart of the world', chapter 4 of *Recovering the Future* (Melbourne, GSES, Monash University, 1988); also revised and expanded in 'Papers: explorations into children's literature', *Magpies Magazine* (Perth, Australia), 2(1), 1991.
10. A selection of concepts, graphic imagery and associated ideas is presented in R. Slaughter, *Futures Concepts and Powerful Ideas* (Melbourne, Futures Study Centre, 1991).
11. For a fine overview of Hampson's work, see A. Crompton, *The Man Who Drew Tomorrow* (Bournemouth, UK, Who Dares Publications, 1985).
12. *Hajime Sorayama* (Berlin, Taco, 1989). These images seem to have taken root in at least two different contexts – wall posters and commercial advertising.
13. Personal communication from Tetsuta Hanamura, Teisei Corp, Japan, October, 1990.
14. I. F. Clarke, *The Pattern Of Expectation* (London, Cape, 1979).
15. A. Asimov and J. Cote, *Future Days* (London, Virgin, 1986).
16. R. Jungk and N. Mullert, *Future Workshops* (London, Institute for Social Inventions, 1987).
17. N. Wilson, 'Young people's vision of our world', *Peace Dossier, 13* (Melbourne, Victorian Association for Peace Studies, September 1985), page 1.
18. See, for example, R. Eckersley, *Australian Attitudes to Science and Technology* (Melbourne, Commission for the Future, 1987).
19. J. Macy, *Despair and Personal Power in the Nuclear Age* (Philadelphia, PA, New Society Publications, 1983).
20. Notes from 'Psychological and spiritual resources for healing our world', Macy intensive seminar, Conishead Priory, Cumbria, UK, 1987.
21. J. Seed, et al, *Thinking Like a Mountain* (Philadelphia, PA, New Society Publications, 1988).
22. See K. Wilber, *Up From Eden: A Transpersonal View of Human Evolution* (London, Routledge and Kegan Paul, 1983).
23. See L. Mumford, *The Pentagon of Power* (London, Secker and Warburg, 1971), pages 172–173.
24. See Wilber, *op cit*, reference 22.

25. T. Berry, *The Dream of the Earth* (San Francisco, CA, Sierra Club, 1988).
26. B. McKibben, *The End of Nature* (Harmondsworth, UK, Penguin, 1990).
27. L. Milbrath, *Envisioning Sustainability with Life Quality* (pamphlet, Buffalo, NY, SUNY, 1989).
28. M. Findlay, 'Imagine the future', Discussion Paper (Imagine the Future Project, Melbourne, September 1990), page 2.
29. Seed, *op cit*, reference 21, page 88.

Chapter 5

1. Bulfinch, T. (1947). *Bulfinch's mythology.* New York: Thomas Y. Crowell.
2. Munch, P. A. (1926). *Norse mythology: Legends of gods and heroes* (S. Bernhardt, Trans.; rev. by M. Olsen). New York: American Scandinavian Foundation.
3. Chang, C. Y. (Trans.). (1975). *Tao: A new way of thinking.* New York: Harper Colophon.
4. Watt, W. M. (1968). *What is Islam?* New York: Praeger.
5. UNESCO. (1980). *Peace on earth: A peace anthology.* Paris: Author.
6. Boulding, E. (1976). *The underside of history: A view of women through time.* Boulder, CO: Westview Press.
7. Lifton, R. (1982). *Indefensible weapons: The political and psychological case against nuclearism.* New York: Basic Books.
8. Kelman, H. (Ed.). (1965). *International behavior: A social-psychological analysis.* New York: Holt, Rinehart & Winston.
9. Lifton, R. (1967). *Death in life: Survivors of Hiroshima.* New York: Random House.
10. White, R. K. (Ed.). (1986). *Psychology and the prevention of nuclear war.* New York: New York University Press.
11. Lifton, R. (1976). *The life of the self: Toward a new psychology.* New York: Simon & Schuster/Touchstone.
12. Lifton, R. (1979). *The broken connection: On death and the continuity of life.* New York: Touchstone.
13. Polak, F. (1953). *De toekomst is verleden tyd* (2 Vol.). Utrecht: W. de Haan. [Trans. by E. Boulding (1961) as *Image of the future.* Leyden: A. W. Sythoff and New York: Oceana Press.]
14. Boulding, E. (1978). Futuristics and the imaging capacity of the West. In M. Maruyama (Ed.), *Cultures of the future* (pp. 7–31). The Hague: Mouton.
15. Boulding, K. (1956). *The image: Knowledge in life and society.* Ann Arbor: University of Michigan Press.
16. Watkins, M. (1986). *Invisible guests: The development of imaginal dialogues.* Hillsdale, NJ: Analytic Press.
17. Jervis, R. (1976). *Perception and misperception of international politics.* Princeton, NJ: Princeton University Press.
18. White, R. K. (1984). *Fearful warriors: A psychological profile of U.S.-Soviet relations.* New York: Free Press.
19. Deutsch, K. (1966). Changing images of international conflict. *Journal of Social Issues.* 23(1), 91–107.
20. Fiske, S., Pratto, F., & Pavelchak, M. (1983). Citizens' images of nuclear war: Content and consequences. *Journal of Social Issues, 39*(1), 41–65.
21. McClelland, D. C., Atkinson, J. W., Clark, R. A., & Lowell, E. L. (1953). *The achievement motive.* New York: Appleton-Century-Crofts.

22. Atkinson, J. W. (1957). Motivational determinants of risk-taking behavior. *Psychological Review 64*, 359–372.
23. LaBerge, S. (1985). *Lucid dreaming*. New York: Ballantine.
24. Ahsen, A. (1981). Visuality among other senses and the eidetic process. *Journal of Mental Imagery, 5*(1), 19–24.
25. Ziegler, W. (1974). Planning as action: Techniques of inventive planning workshops. In *Participatory planning in education*. Paris: Organization for Economic Cooperation and Development.
26. Ziegler, W. (1985). *A mindbook of imagining and inventing a world without weapons*. Denver, CO: Futures Invention Associates.
27. Jung, C. G. (1959). *The basic writings of Jung*. New York: Modern Library.
28. Chomsky, N. (1966). *Cartesian linguistics: A chapter in the history of rationalist thought*. New York: Harper & Row.
29. Boulding, E. (1979). Deep structures and sociological analysis: Some reflections. *American Sociologist, 14*, 70–73.

INDEX